GRANT
VS.
LEE

THE
GRAPHIC
HISTORY
OF THE CIVIL WAR'S
GREATEST
RIVALS
DURING THE **LAST YEAR**
OF THE WAR

WRITTEN AND ILLUSTRATED BY
WAYNE
VANSANT
AUTHOR OF *GETTYSBURG*

ZENITH PRESS

First published in 2013 by Zenith Press, an imprint of MBI Publishing
Company, 400 First Avenue North, Suite 400, Minneapolis, MN 55401
USA

Zenith Press titles are also available at discounts in bulk
quantity for industrial or sales-promotional use. For details
write to Special Sales Manager at MBI Publishing Company,
400 First Avenue North, Suite 400, Minneapolis, MN 55401 USA.

To find out more about our books, join us online at
www.zenithpress.com.

Library of Congress Cataloging-in-Publication Data

Vansant, Wayne.
    Grant vs. Lee : the graphic history of the Civil War's greatest rivals
during the last year of the war / Wayne Vansant.
      pages cm. — (Zenith graphic histories)
    ISBN 978-0-7603-4531-3 (softcover)
    1. United States—History—Civil War, 1861-1865—Campaigns—
Comic books, strips, etc. 2. United States—History—Civil War, 1861-
1865—Campaigns—Juvenile literature. 3. Virginia—History—Civil
War, 1861-1865—Campaigns—Comic books, strips, etc. 4. Virginia—
History—Civil War, 1861-1865—Campaigns—Juvenile literature. 5.
Grant, Ulysses S. (Ulysses Simpson), 1822-1885—Comic books, strips,
etc. 6. Grant, Ulysses S. (Ulysses Simpson), 1822-1885—Juvenile
literature. 7. Lee, Robert E. (Robert Edward), 1807-1870—Comic
books, strips, etc. 8. Lee, Robert E. (Robert Edward), 1807-1870—
Juvenile literature. 9. Graphic novels. I. Title. II. Title: Grant versus
Lee.
    E470.V36 2013
    973.7'3--dc23
                                        2013017507

Editor: Erik Gilg
Art Director: Rebecca Pagel
Layout: Chris Fayers
Cover Design: Kent Jensen, knail

Printed in China

CONTENTS

GRANT'S OVERLAND CAMPAIGN

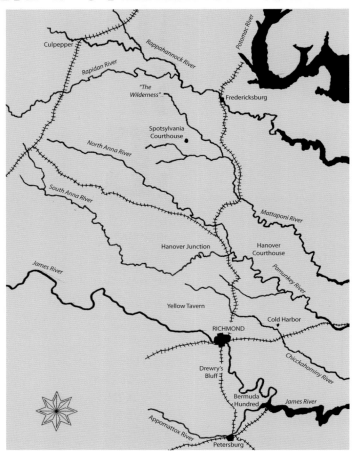

LEE'S RETREAT TO APPOMATTOX

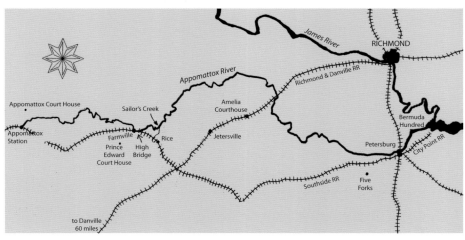

GRANT VS. LEE

SPRING 1864.
BULL RUN. FREDERICKSBURG.
GETTYSBURG. ALL IN THE PAST.
MCCELLAN AND MCDOWELL WERE
GONE. THE WAR OF THE STRATEGIC
AMATEUR WAS OVER. WHAT WAS
TO COME WAS UNLIKE ANYTHING
THE NORTH AND SOUTH HAD SEEN.
UNION GENERAL WILLIAM TECUMSEH
SHERMAN SAID IT BEST IN HIS OWN
HARD, UNCOMPROMISING STYLE:

"WAR, LIKE THE
THUNDERBOLT, FOLLOWS
ITS LAWS AND TURNS
NOT ASIDE, EVEN
IF THE BEAUTIFUL,
THE VIRTUOUS, AND
CHARITABLE STAND IN
ITS PATH."

ACROSS THE RAPIDAN

THURSDAY, MARCH 10, 1864. BRANDY STATION, VIRGINIA, HEADQUARTERS OF THE ARMY OF THE POTOMAC. A REGIMENT OF ZOUAVES AND THE HEADQUARTERS' BAND WAITED IN A DRIVING RAIN TO GREET THE NEW COMMANDER OF ALL UNION FORCES.

HE WAS LT. GEN. ULYSSES SIMPSON GRANT, AGE 41, VICTOR OF FORT DONELSON AND VICKSBURG. HE WAS THERE TO MEET WITH LT. GENERAL GEORGE MEADE, WHO HAD COMMANDED THE ARMY OF THE POTOMAC SINCE JUST BEFORE THE BATTLE OF GETTYSBURG IN THE SUMMER OF 1863.

IT WAS GRANT'S INTENTION TO REMOVE MEADE FROM HIS POST, BUT WHEN HE MET THE 48-YEAR-OLD SPANISH-BORN GENERAL, HE WAS COMPLETELY DISARMED BY HIS HUMILITY AND HONESTY.

"THE WORK BEFORE US IS OF SUCH VAST IMPORTANCE . . . THAT THE FEELINGS OR WISHES OF NO PERSON SHOULD STAND IN THE WAY OF SELECTING THE RIGHT MAN FOR ALL POSITIONS."

MEADE EXPECTED GRANT TO REPLACE HIM IMMEDIATELY, POSSIBLY WITH MAJ. GEN. WILLIAM TECUMSEH SHERMAN, WHO WAS GRANT'S RIGHT HAND IN THE WESTERN CAMPAIGNS. BUT AFTER MEETING MEADE, GRANT WAS IMPRESSED AND TOLD HIM THAT HE HAD NO INTENSION OF REPLACING HIM. NOW IT WAS MEADE WHO WAS IMPRESSED.

THE NEXT DAY GRANT TOOK A TRAIN TO CINCINNATI, OHIO, TO MEET WITH SHERMAN AND PLAN THE CAMPAIGN THAT WOULD BEGIN THAT SPRING.

GRANT AND SHERMAN CHECKED INTO THE BURNET HOUSE HOTEL. FOR THE NEXT TWO DAYS, OVER WHISKEY AND CIGARS, THEY PLANNED THE GREAT OFFENSIVE THAT THEY HOPED WOULD BRING THE CONFEDERACY TO ITS KNEES. IN MAY, SHERMAN, WITH NEARLY 100,000 MEN, WOULD BEGIN HIS ADVANCE AGAINST ATLANTA, AN IMPORTANT COMMERCIAL AND RAILROAD CENTER IN THE SOUTH. AT THE SAME TIME, GRANT WOULD BEGIN HIS MARCH ON RICHMOND WITH 122,000 MEN FROM THE ARMY OF THE POTOMAC. ONCE THE ADVANCE BEGAN, THERE WOULD BE NO STOPPING IT. THEY BELIEVED THAT THE POPULATION AND THE MATERIAL WEALTH OF THE NORTH WOULD BE ABLE TO SUSTAIN THE LOSSES THEY WOULD INCUR. THE SOUTH, ON THE OTHER HAND, WOULD NOT BE ABLE TO REPLACE ITS LOSSES.

IN VIRGINIA, GRANT WOULD HAVE TWO OTHER ARMIES TO SUPPORT HIM. MAJOR GENERAL FRANZ SIGEL, WITH 26,000 MEN, WOULD ADVANCE UP THE SHENANDOAH VALLEY. MAJOR GENERAL L BENJAMIN BUTLER'S ARMY OF THE JAMES WOULD MARCH UP THE VIRGINIA PENINSULA, THE FINGER OF LAND BETWEEN THE YORK AND JAMES RIVERS, TOWARD RICHMOND, LINKING UP WITH THE ARMY OF THE POTOMAC WHEN POSSIBLE.

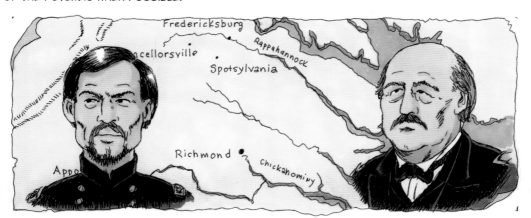

WHEN GRANT RETURNED TO VIRGINIA, HE MADE IT CLEAR TO MEADE WHAT HIS JOB WOULD BE ONCE THE OFFENSIVE BEGAN: "LEE'S ARMY WILL BE YOUR OBJECTIVE POINT. WHEREVER LEE GOES, THERE YOU WILL GO ALSO."

ON MARCH 29, GRANT WENT TO REVIEW THE PROUD TROOPS OF GOUVERNEUR KEMBLE WARREN'S V CORPS.

A COLONEL OF ARTILLERY NOTED: "HE RODE ALONG THE LINE IN A SLOUCHY UNOBSERVANT WAY, WITH HIS COAT UNBUTTONED AND SETTING ANYTHING BUT AN EXAMPLE OF MILITARY BEARING TO THE TROOPS."

GRANT'S REPUTATION PRECEDED HIM, YET MOST SOLDIERS WERE STILL A BIT SKEPTICAL. THE UNION'S MEN HAD SEEN LOTS OF GENERALS: MCDOWELL, MCCLELLAN, POPE, BURNSIDE, HOOKER. THEY HAD HEARD ALL ABOUT GRANT'S EXPLOITS OUT WEST . . .

. . . BUT HE HAD YET TO MEET BOBBY LEE AND HIS BOYS.

AND SO HE DID. THE UNION ADVANCE BEGAN ON WEDNESDAY, MAY 4, AS THREE OF THE CORPS BEGAN TO CROSS OVER NEWLY CONSTRUCTED PONTOON BRIDGES. WATCHING THE CROSSING, AN OFFICER ON MEADE'S STAFF NOTED IN HIS DIARY, "HOW STRANGE IT WOULD BE IF EACH MAN WHO WAS DESTINED TO FALL IN THE CAMPAIGN AHEAD HAD SOME LARGE BADGE ON." HE HAD NO WAY OF KNOWING, BUT ALMOST HALF WOULD BE WEARING SUCH A BADGE.

GRANT HIMSELF CROSSED AT NOON, RIDING HIS BIG BAY, CINCINNATI. WITH HIM WAS CONGRESSMAN ELIHU B. WASHBURNE OF ILLINOIS. SOLDIERS WHO SAW THE TWO MEN RIDING TOGETHER SPECULATED ON WHO LEE'S PARTNER WAS. THEY FINALLY DECIDED IT WAS GRANT'S PERSONAL UNDERTAKER.

LATE THAT AFTERNOON, THE ARMY OF THE POTOMAC HALTED TO CAMP IN A JUNGLE-LIKE STRETCH OF SECOND-GROWTH TIMBER AND ISOLATED FARMS KNOWN LOCALLY AS THE WILDERNESS. HERE, ONE YEAR BEFORE, WAS WHERE THE BATTLE OF CHANCELLORSVILLE TOOK PART. THERE WERE THE SKELETONS OF THAT BATTLE EVERYWHERE, UNCOVERED BY THE WINTER RAINS.

THEIR BLACK, EMPTY EYES SEEMED TO SAY, "THIS IS WHAT YOU ARE ALL COMING TO, AND SOME OF YOU WILL START TOWARD IT TOMORROW." THE CONFEDERATE ARMY SET UP CAMP ONLY TWO MILES AWAY.

INTO THE WILDERNESS

BATTLE OF THE WILDERNESS

BY 7 AM, THE CORPS OF WINFIELD SCOTT HANCOCK AND GOUVERNEUR KEMBLE WARREN WERE STRUNG OUT ALONG ISOLATED COUNTRY ROADS WHEN FEDERAL SKIRMISHERS ENCOUNTERED SOME CONFEDERATE INFANTRY.

THESE TROOPS WERE PART OF ONE-LEGGED RICHARD EWELL'S CORPS. LEE ORDERED EWELL TO "GO STRAIGHT DOWN THE ROAD AND STRIKE THE ENEMY WHEREVER YOU FIND HIM."

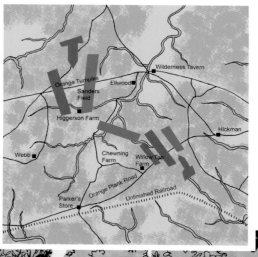

IN THIS CONGESTED LANDSCAPE, NEITHER SIDE COULD BRING ITS FULL FORCE AGAINST THE ENEMY. THEY MANEUVERED FOR HOURS UNTIL, FINALLY, THE FIGHT BEGAN.

THE FIGHT TOOK PLACE IN TWO LOCATIONS: ONE AROUND A LARGE, BRAMBLE-COVERED CLEARING CALLED SANDER'S FIELD, WHICH SAT ON BOTH SIDES OF THE ORANGE–FREDERICKSBURG TURNPIKE AND IT PITTED EWELL'S CORPS AGAINST WARREN'S FEDERAL V CORPS. THE OTHER CLASH WOULD BE TWO MILES TO THE SOUTHEAST BETWEEN THE CONFEDERATES OF A. P. HILL'S CORPS AND HANCOCK'S AND SEDGWICK'S CORPS.

BY NOON, TWO OF WARREN'S DIVISIONS ADVANCED AGAINST EWELL. LEE ORDERED EWELL TO AVOID A GENERAL ENGAGEMENT UNTIL LONGSTREET'S CORPS HAD ARRIVED.

THE BRISK FEDERAL ADVANCE, HOWEVER, LEFT EWELL LITTLE CHOICE. THE BATTLE TOOK A LIFE OF ITS OWN. THE DIVISION OF UNION BRIG. GEN. CHARLES GRIFFIN BEGAN TO ADVANCE THROUGH THE THICKETS USING THE TURNPIKE AS A GUIDE.

IN THE VANGUARD OF THE ADVANCE WERE THE 140TH AND 146TH NEW YORK ZOUAVES REGIMENTS. THEY ADVANCED ACROSS SANDER'S FIELD THROUGH MATTED BRAMBLES, TANGLED BRUSH, AND ACROSS HIDDEN GULLIES. THEIR REINFORCEMENTS GOT CONFUSED IN THE UNDERGROWTH.

MEN BECAME CONFUSED AND DISORIENTED AND FLANKS OPENED UP. EWELL COUNTERATTACKED. THE ZOUAVES FELL BACK, REORGANIZED, AND MARCHED FORWARD WITH SHOUTS THAT DROWNED OUT ALL OTHER SOUNDS.

THE WOODS AND FOREST SUDDENLY CAUGHT FIRE AND THE FLAMES SPREAD TO THE BRAMBLE-CHOKED FIELD.

SOON, THE SCREAMS OF THE WOUNDED COULD BE HEARD AMID THE SOUND OF BATTLE. THOSE TOO HURT TO FLEE ON FOOT WERE ENGULFED IN THE APPROACHING FLAMES.

TWO MILES TO THE SOUTHEAST, THE REBELS AND YANKEES WERE STRUGGLING OVER THE CROSSROADS OF THE ORANGE PLANK AND BROCK ROADS. LEE SENT OUT UNITS TO TIE IN WITH EWELL TO HIS LEFT AND PREPARED A FULL-SCALE ATTACK ON THE CROSSROADS.

A LITTLE AFTER 4 PM, THE 7,000 CONFEDERATES UNDER MAJ. GEN. HENRY HETH MET THE 17,000 FEDERALS OF BRIG. GEN. RICHARD GETTY WHO WERE ADVANCING FROM THE CROSSROADS. THE SOUTHERNERS QUICKLY BUILT LIGHT BREASTWORK TO PROVIDE PROTECTION FROM THE ENEMY.

THE CONFEDERATE FIRE CUT DOWN THE UNION ADVANCE AS THE SOLDIERS TOPPED A WOODED RIDGE 50 YARDS IN FRONT OF THEM. SOON THE FIRE WAS SO HEAVY FROM BOTH SIDES THAT BOTH SIDES WENT TO EARTH, KEEPING UP THEIR FIRE FROM PRONE POSITIONS.

THE SOUTHERNERS SOON LEARNED THAT A UNION FORCE WAS APPROACHING THROUGH THE HEAVY WOODS TO THE CONFEDERATE LEFT. A. P. HILL SENT THE ONLY MEN HE HAD TO SPARE, A BATTALION FROM THE 5TH ALABAMA, WHO HAD BEEN HELD BACK TO GUARD PRISONERS.

THE 125 ALABAMIANS FROM THE 5TH HIT THE BLUE-CLAD MEN IN THE DENSE FOREST WITH FORCE, AND SCREAMED THE REBEL YELL WITH SUCH ENTHUSIASM THAT THE UNION LINE WAS CONVINCED THERE WERE MORE OF THEM THAN THEIR ACTUAL NUMBERS. THEIR WILD ATTACK STOPPED THE FEDERAL ADVANCE BUT COULD NOT MAKE THEM WITHDRAW.

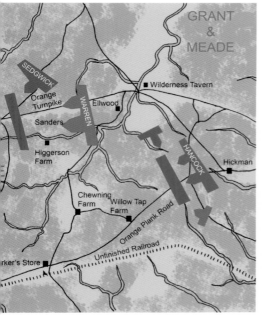

THE FIGHTING ESCALATED SLIGHTLY ON EWELL'S FRONT BEFORE IT DIED DOWN AS NIGHT APPROACHED. WITH DARKNESS CAME THE SOUND OF AXES, AND MEN USED THE NIGHT COVER TO IMPROVE THEIR POSITIONS. WITH DARKNESS ALSO CAME THE CRIES OF THE WOUNDED, WHICH SOON BECAME SCREAMS AS THE MANY FIRES ENGULFED THEM. MEN FROM BOTH ARMIES SLEPT WHEREVER THEY COULD.

BOTH SIDES PLANNED ATTACKS FOR EARLY THE NEXT MORNING.

BY MORNING, THE BATTLE RESUMED. 20,000 FEDERALS FROM HANCOCK'S CORPS SLAMMED INTO A. P. HILL'S FRONT.

BY 7 AM THE FEDERALS PUSHED THE CONFEDERATES BACK A MILE OR SO.

LEE HIMSELF RALLIED THE BRIGADE OF BRIG. GEN. SAMUEL MCGOWAN, AND THE UNION ADVANCE BEGAN TO SLOW.

AT THIS PIVOTAL MOMENT, LONGSTREET'S CORPS ARRIVED. HIS MEN CAME PUSHING THROUGH THE WRECKAGE OF HILL'S CORPS AND FORMED THEMSELVES, READY TO FIGHT.

THE TEXAS BRIGADE ARRIVED TO THE FRONT. THEY WERE LEE'S OLD SHOCK TROOPS, NOW UNDER THE COMMAND OF BRIG. GEN. JOHN GREGG. "HURRAH FOR TEXAS!" LEE YELLED OUT, FOR HE KNEW THESE MEN WELL. "HURRAH FOR TEXAS! TEXANS ALWAYS MOVE THEM!"

THE TEXANS CUT THROUGH THE WOODS WITH RECKLESS FORCE AND BY MIDMORNING THEY HAD PUSHED THE UNION ATTACK ALMOST BACK TO THE POINT WHERE IT HAD STARTED.

LONGSTREET DISCOVERED A GAP IN THE UNION LINE. HE SENT FOUR BRIGADES UP AN UNFINISHED RAILROAD CUT. AT 11 AM THEY EMERGED FROM THE CUT UNSEEN.

THEY HIT THE SURPRISED FEDERALS BEFORE THEY COULD FORM UP PROPERLY TO FIGHT. IN NO TIME AT ALL, THE CONFEDERATES HIT HANCOCK'S LINE HARD.

DURING THE CONFUSION OF THE ADVANCE, CONFEDERATE SOLDIERS RECONNOITERING THE FRONT MISTAKENLY FIRED AT LONGSTREET AND SEVERAL OTHER CONFEDERATE OFFICERS.

THREE OFFICERS WERE KILLED AND LONGSTREET WAS WOUNDED THROUGH THE NECK, BUT NOT CRITICALLY. IN FACT, IT WAS TO CLOSE TO THIS VERY SPOT THAT STONEWALL JACKSON WAS ACCIDENTLY MORTALLY WOUNDED BY HIS OWN MEN A YEAR EARLIER.

AIDED BY FIRE AND SMOKE THAT WAS FLOWING AGAINST THE YANKS, THE SOUTHERN ADVANCE REACHED THE FEDERAL BREASTWORKS BEFORE BEING THROWN BACK.

ON EWELL'S FRONT, THE GEORGIANS OF BRIG. GEN. JOHN B. GORDON BROKE THE FEDERAL RIGHT FLANK. BEFORE DARKNESS PUT AN END TO THEIR ATTACK, THEY INFLICTED 400 CASUALTIES AND CAPTURED SEVERAL HUNDRED MEN, INCLUDING TWO BRIGADIER GENERALS.

LEE LOST 7,500 CASUALTIES IN TWO DAYS, AND GRANT LOST 17,666, AND STILL THEY HAD NOT FOUGHT CLEAR OF THE WILDERNESS.

BEFORE RETIRING TO HIS TENT THAT NIGHT, GRANT SPOKE TO A CORRESPONDENT WHO WAS ABOUT TO DEPART FOR WASHINGTON, D.C. "IF YOU SEE THE PRESIDENT," GRANT SAID, "TELL HIM, FOR ME, THAT WHATEVER HAPPENS, THERE WILL BE NO TURNING BACK."

IT WAS BECOMING CLEAR THAT GRANT INTENDED TO PURSUE LEE WITHOUT PAUSE. THE BATTLES WOULD NO LONGER BE STORMS SEPARATED BY CALM WHERE THE ARMIES LICKED THEIR WOUNDS. FROM NOW ON IT WOULD BE A CONSTANT THUNDER.

AT 6 PM ON MAY 10, FEDERAL ARTILLERY OPENED UP ON THE CONFEDERATE DEFENSES.

10 MINUTES LATER, 5,000 MEN FROM 12 VETERAN REGIMENTS CHARGED TOWARD THE MULE SHOE.

THEY WERE COMMANDED BY 24-YEAR-OLD EMORY UPTON, WHO HAD BEEN PREACHING A NEW THEORY OF ATTACK: A HAMMER BLOW BY A CONCENTRATED STRIKING FORCE HITTING A NARROW POINT OF THE ENEMY DEFENSES. ONCE THE LINE HAD BEEN BREECHED, THE ATTACKERS WOULD POUR THROUGH AND ROLL UP THE FLANKS.

WITHIN FIVE MINUTES THE FASTEST MEN HAD MADE THEIR WAY THROUGH THE ABATIS.

THE FEDERALS WERE THEN ON THE EDGE OF THE TRENCH AND WERE POURING FIRE INTO THE SURPRISED DEFENDERS.

A GEORGIA REGIMENT ABSOLUTELY REFUSED TO GIVE WAY.

NUMBERS, HOWEVER, SOON PREVAILED.

UPTON'S MEN POURED THROUGH THE GAP AND BEGAN TO WIDEN IT. SO FAR, THE PLAN HAD WORKED. BUT TO HOLD THE GAP OPEN, UPTON NEEDED REINFORCEMENTS.

TWENTY TWO CONFEDERATE CANNONS, HOWEVER, KEPT THE FEDERAL REINFORCEMENTS FROM SUPPORTING UPTON.

UPTON HAD NO CHOICE BUT TO WITHDRAW HIS FORCES. UNDER THE COVER OF DARKNESS, THE 12 REGIMENTS PULLED BACK TO THEIR LINES, TAKING 950 CONFEDERATE PRISONERS WITH THEM.

UPTON'S FORCES SUFFERED ABOUT 1,000 CASUALTIES, BUT IN GRANT'S MIND THE YOUNG COLONEL'S TACTICS WERE SOUND. HE PROMOTED UPTON TO BRIGADIER GENERAL. GRANT WAS HEARD SAYING TO GENERAL MEADE THAT NIGHT, "A BRIGADE TODAY, WE'LL TRY A CORPS TOMORROW."

GORDON'S DESPERATE ATTACK SLAMMED INTO HANCOCK'S ADVANCING TROOPS, CAUSING THEM TO STAGGER AND LOSE MOMENTUM. THE MULE SHOE WAS FILLING UP WITH A MASS OF FIGHTING, CURSING, AND DYING MEN.

ARTILLERY WAS BROUGHT IN AND USED AT EXTREMELY CLOSE RANGE, AND THE EFFECT WAS BRUTAL.

OTHERS FOUGHT WITH PISTOLS, BAYONETS, KNIVES, THEIR FISTS, OR WHATEVER WAS AT HAND.

BRIGADIER GENERAL STEPHEN DODSON RAMSEUR'S NORTH CAROLINA BRIGADE SURGED FORWARD. RAMSEUR, HAVING HAD HIS HORSE SHOT OUT FROM UNDER HIM AND HIMSELF WOUNDED IN THE RIGHT ARM, STILL LED HIS MEN FORWARD, AS ONE MAN PUT IT, "LIKE AN ANGEL OF WAR."

NOT ONLY OFFICERS INSPIRED. PRIVATE TISDALE STEPP STARTED SINGING "THE BONNIE BLUE FLAG" AT THE TOP OF HIS LUNGS. SOON THE ENTIRE 14TH NORTH CAROLINA WAS BELTING OUT THE STIRRING SOUTHERN ANTHEM AS IT POURED FIRE INTO THE FOE.

THE FIGHT LASTED MORE THAN 10 HOURS AND GAVE THE MULE SHOE ANOTHER NAME: THE BLOODY ANGLE. CONFEDERATE ENGINEERS WERE BUSY CONSTRUCTING ANOTHER LINE OF TRENCHES AT THE BASE OF THE SALIENT, BUT THE SOUTHERNERS HAD TO HOLD OUT UNTIL THEY WERE COMPLETED AROUND MIDNIGHT.

THE NEXT MORNING, MAY 13, THE FEDERAL SOLDIERS FOUND THE TRENCHES OF THE MULE SHOE EMPTY—EXCEPT, THAT IS, FOR THE DEAD.

BOTH SIDES LOST ABOUT 10,000 MEN DEAD, WOUNDED, OR CAPTURED IN THIS INCONCLUSIVE BATTLE.

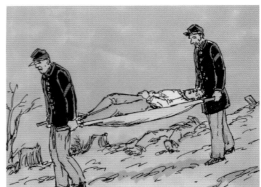

GRANT PUT THE BEST FACE HE COULD ON THE SITUATION AND BEGAN MOVING HIS FORCES SLOWLY TO THE EAST, TRYING TO SLIP PAST LEE'S FLANK. LEE, HOWEVER, WOULD COUNTER EVERY MOVE. A FIGHT OF SOME SORT WOULD TAKE PLACE EVERY DAY AT SPOTSYLVANIA FOR THE NEXT WEEK. SOON, AS ON DOZENS OF OTHER BATTLEFIELDS, THE ARMIES MOVED AWAY, LEAVING ONLY THE SCARRED GROUND AND TREES . . . AND THE DEAD.

MOVE AND COUNTER MOVE

GRANT HAD LOST 36,065 MEN SINCE MAY 5. ANOTHER 14,000 HAD DESERTED OR GONE HOME WHEN THEIR ENLISTMENTS WERE UP. UNFORTUNATELY, ONLY 12,000 REPLACEMENTS WERE AVAILABLE.

THINGS WERE LOOKING UP FOR THE SOUTH. IN THE SHENANDOAH VALLEY, CONFEDERATE FORCES OF MAJ. GEN. JOHN BRECKINRIDGE HAD ROUTED MAJ. GEN. FRANZ SIGEL'S UNION FORCES AT NEW MARKET. THIS ALLOWED BRECKINRIDGE TO SEND 2,500 MEN TO REINFORCE LEE.

IN ADDITION, P. G. T. BEAUREGARD'S CONFEDERATE FORCES HAD CORNERED BEN BUTLER'S ARMY OF THE JAMES IN A LOOP OF THE JAMES RIVER CALLED THE BERMUDA HUNDRED. WITH THIS ACHIEVEMENT, BEAUREGARD WAS ABLE TO SEND A DIVISION OF 6,000 MEN TO LEE.

DESPITE THESE FACTS GRANT STILL FELT CONFIDENT AND BELIEVED HE WAS FOLLOWING THE RIGHT COURSE. EVEN THOUGH THERE HAD BEEN HEAVY RAINS THAT HAD TURNED THE ROADS INTO A HUGE MESS, GRANT BEGAN TO SLOWLY PULL HIS MEN OUT OF THE LINE FACING THE CONFEDERATE'S BREASTWORKS AT SPOTSYLVANIA AND SHIFT THEM TO THE LEFT, TRYING TO TURN LEE'S RIGHT.

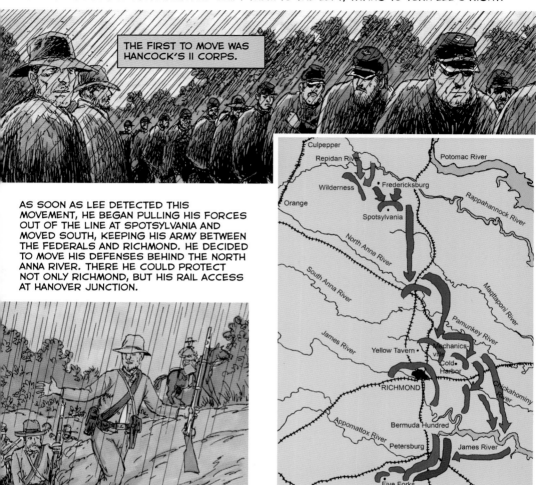

THE FIRST TO MOVE WAS HANCOCK'S II CORPS.

AS SOON AS LEE DETECTED THIS MOVEMENT, HE BEGAN PULLING HIS FORCES OUT OF THE LINE AT SPOTSYLVANIA AND MOVED SOUTH, KEEPING HIS ARMY BETWEEN THE FEDERALS AND RICHMOND. HE DECIDED TO MOVE HIS DEFENSES BEHIND THE NORTH ANNA RIVER. THERE HE COULD PROTECT NOT ONLY RICHMOND, BUT HIS RAIL ACCESS AT HANOVER JUNCTION.

ONCE BEHIND THE NORTH ANNA BANKS, LEE WANTED HIS MEN TO REST FROM THE MANY DAYS FIGHTING. THEY COULD REST EASILY ENOUGH, BUT THE CONFEDERATE COMMISSARY COULD NOT PROVIDE THEM WITH ENOUGH FOOD. A REGULAR DAY'S RATIONS WAS ONE PINT OF UNSIFTED CORNMEAL AND 1/4 POUND OF BACON.

THE ARMY OF NORTHERN VIRGINIA ALSO NEEDED REST AND RECOUPMENT. LONGSTREET WAS STILL SUFFERING FROM HIS WOUNDS AND EWELL WAS SHOWING SIGNS OF PHYSICAL COLLAPSE. A. P. HILL WAS SUFFERING FROM A CHRONIC AILMENT THAT HAD BEEN AFFECTING HIM SINCE HIS DAYS AT WEST POINT.

LEE WAS ALSO SUFFERING FROM A BAD CASE OF DIARRHEA. THE NORMALLY COURTLY COMMANDER DIDN'T SEEM HIMSELF AND HE WAS IMPATIENT AND CROSS WITH EVERYONE.

THE ARMY OF THE POTOMAC BEGAN TO CROSS THE NORTH ANNA ON MAY 23. LEE'S POSITION MADE IT DIFFICULT FOR GRANT TO COORDINATE AN EFFECTIVE ATTACK. GRANT'S ATTEMPTS WEREN'T VERY BLOODY, BUT STILL TOO COSTLY CONSIDERING THE MINIMAL GAINS.

SO AS HE HAD BEFORE, GRANT BEGAN TO MOVE HIS ARMY EAST ON MAY 26. TWO DAYS LATER, LEE WAS COMPELLED TO FOLLOW HIM, ALWAYS POSITIONING HIMSELF AND HIS ARMY BETWEEN GRANT AND RICHMOND. "WE MUST DESTROY THIS ARMY OF GRANT'S BEFORE HE GETS TO THE JAMES RIVER," LEE TOLD GEN. JUBAL EARLY, WHO WOULD SOON REPLACE THE SICKLY EWELL. "IF HE GETS THERE IT WILL BECOME A SIEGE, AND THEN IT WILL BE A MERE QUESTION OF TIME."

LEE RUSHED HIS FORCES SOUTH AND EAST, FINALLY GETTING BACK IN FRONT OF GRANT AT COLD HARBOR, SETTING THE STAGE FOR ONE OF THE WAR'S BLOODIEST AND COSTLIEST BATTLES.

MURDER AT COLD HARBOR BATTLE OF COLD HARBOR

THROUGH THE END OF MAY, GRANT'S FORCES STAYED ON THE MARCH, ALWAYS MOVING SOUTHEAST, ALWAYS TRYING TO FLANK LEE'S ARMY AND GET BETWEEN THE CONDFEDERATE FORCES AND RICHMOND.

THE REBS KEPT MOVING TOO, ALWAYS GETTING IN GRANT'S WAY, ALWAYS READY TO BUILD A MAKESHIFT BREASTWORKS AT MOMENT'S NOTICE TO FIGHT. BUT THEY KNEW THAT THEY COULD NOT FIGHT AN OPEN BATTLE THE WAY THEY HAD IN THE PAST. THERE WERE TOO FEW OF THEM AND TOO MANY YANKEES. THEY WOULD HAVE TO CHOOSE THEIR GROUND WELL.

BECAUSE THEY WERE IN THE "INTERIOR" OF GRANT'S MOVEMENT, THEY DIDN'T HAVE AS FAR TO TRAVEL AS THEIR ENEMY. THIS WAS A DISTINCT ADVANTAGE , BECAUSE THEY DIDN'T WEAR THEMSELVES OUT AS MUCH AS THE NORTHERNERS.

THEY HAD A BIG PROBLEM, THOUGH. THEY WERE ON THE BRINK OF STARVATION. SOME MEN HADN'T HAD RATIONS FOR TWO DAYS. LEE KNEW THE SITUATION WAS CRITICAL. HE HAD TO SLOW GRANT DOWN AND SOMEHOW FEED HIS ARMY.

WHEN THE ORDER TO FIRE WAS GIVEN, THE FIRST FEDERAL ADVANCING LINE WAS TORN TO PIECES.

THE SURVIVORS TRIED TO TURN AND FLEE BUT WERE STOPPED BY THE BAYONETS, GUN BUTTS, AND SWORDS OF THE SECOND FEDERAL LINE WHO WERE RIGHT BEHIND THEM.

THIS MADE THE SECOND LINE AN EVEN EASIER TARGET.

IN THE CONFEDERATE TRENCHES, GEN. EVANDER LAW FOUND "THE MEN IN FINE SPIRITS, LAUGHING AND TALKING AS THEY FIRED."

BUT WHEN LAW SAW THE CARNAGE IN FRONT OF HIM, HE THOUGHT, "IT WAS NOT WAR; IT WAS MURDER."

SOME OF THE HEAVIEST FIGHTING WAS ON THE EXTREME LEFT OF THE UNION LINE, HELD BY HANCOCK'S II CORPS.

THERE FRANCIS BARLOW'S DIVISION FOUND A WEAK SPOT IN THE CONFEDERATE WORKS.

UNDER BARLOW'S COMMAND WAS THE 7TH NEW YORK HEAVY ARTILLERY, WHICH SPENT MOST OF THE WAR GUARDING WASHINGTON, D.C. NOW THESE SOLDIERS WERE FIGHTING AS INFANTRYMEN AND THEY NOW MANAGED TO FIGHT THEIR WAY INTO THE NEAREST PARAPET. INSIDE IT THEY CAPTURED 200 CONFEDERATES, TWO CANNONS, AND A STAND OF COLORS.

NEW YORK'S LEFT LINE WAS BREACHED, BUT BY NOW THE TIDE HAD TURNED. THE HARD-FIGHTING CONFEDERATE 2ND MARYLAND AND A FLORIDA BRIGADE UNDER THE COMMAND OF A TOUGH, IRISH-BORN BRIG. GEN. JOSEPH FINEGAN PUSHED THE FEDERALS OUT OF THE LINE.

MOST OF BARLOW'S MEN WERE CUT DOWN BEFORE THEY GOT A GOOD LOOK AT THE CONFEDERATE TRENCHES.

JOHN GIBBON'S DIVISION SUFFERED JUST AS BADLY.

CONFEDERATE ARTILLERY BLEW HUGE HOLES IN THE CLOSELY PACKED UNION ADVANCE.

HORATIO G. WRIGHT'S VI CORPS ALSO SUFFERED HEAVILY DESPITE THE EXTREME RANGE OF THE REBEL RIFLE FIRE.

WILLIAM SMITH'S XVIII CORPS HAD THE ADVANTAGE OF TERRAIN AND GOOD RECONNAISSANCE. A STREAM BANK ALLOWED HIM AND HIS MEN TO ADVANCE TOWARD THE CONFEDERATE LINE UNDER PARTIAL COVER.

STILL, THE REBEL FIRE PILED UP THE UNION DEAD LIKE CORDWOOD.

BY 5:30 AM, THOSE STILL ALIVE IN FRONT OF THE CONFEDERATE WORKS HUGGED THE EARTH. THERE WERE AS MANY AS 7,000 CASUALTIES THROUGHOUT THE DAY, MOST OF THEM IN THE FIRST QUARTER HOUR OF THE ATTACK.

LEE WAS SLOW TO GRASP WHAT HAD JUST HAPPENED. THE SHEER QUANTITY OF THE DEAD BEFORE THEIR LINES SHOCKED EVEN THE MOST SEASONED VETERANS. COLONEL CHARLES VENABLE SUMMED IT UP BEST: COLD HARBOR WAS "PERHAPS THE EASIEST VICTORY EVER GRANTED TO THE CONFEDERATE ARMS BY THE FOLLY OF THE FEDERAL COMMANDERS."

CONFEDERATE LOSSES WERE ABOUT 1,500 MEN.

36

GRANT AND MEADE WERE SLOW TO UNDERSTAND THE FULL PICTURE OF THE CARNAGE, SO THEY ORDERED THE ATTACK TO CONTINUE.

FOR THE MEN WHO LIVED THROUGH THE SLAUGHTER, THIS SEEMED RIDICULOUS AND WAS WIDELY ACKNOWLEDGED FROM THE CORPS COMMANDERS RIGHT DOWN TO THE LOWEST PRIVATE.

AS THE MORNING PROGRESSED THERE WAS SCATTERED RIFLE AND CANNON FIRE, BUT FOR THE MOST PART, THE CRIES OF THE WOUNDED WERE MAINLY HEARD. THE FEDERALS COULD NOT GET TO THEIR FALLEN COMRADES AND NEITHER SIDE WOULD AGREE TO A CEASEFIRE BECAUSE THAT WOULD SIGNAL DEFEAT.

SOME BELIEVED GRANT'S REFUSAL TO CALL A TRUCE HAD POLITICAL MOTIVATION. IF WORD OF A DEFEAT GOT OUT, IT WOULD AID THE RESISTANCE TO THE WAR IN THE NORTH.

MANY ALSO WONDERED IF LINCOLN WOULD HAVE RECEIVED HIS SECOND NOMINATION FROM THE REPUBLICAN PARTY IF THE NEWS OF THE SLAUGHTER HAD BEEN MADE PUBLIC.

BY THE TIME THE MEDICAL TEAMS AND BURIAL PARTIES FINALLY WENT OUT EIGHT DAYS LATER ON JUNE 7, IT NO LONGER MATTERED. MOST OF THE WOUNDED WERE DEAD.

OPPORTUNITIES MISSED

COLD HARBOR, LATE EVENING, JUNE 12, 1864. FOR THE CONFEDERATES ON PICKET DUTY, NOTHING SEEMED UNUSUAL AS THEY WAITED FOR THE YANKS TO DECIDE WHAT THEY WERE GOING TO DO NEXT.

BUT THIS WAS NO ORDINARY NIGHT. THE ARMY OF THE POTOMAC WAS ON THE MOVE. MORE THAN 100,000 MEN, FIVE INFANTRY CORPS, ONE DIVISION OF CAVALRY, AND 49 ARTILLERY BATTERIES, ALONG WITH 1,200 CAISSONS OF AMMUNITION AND AN ENORMOUS TRAIN OF SUPPLY WAGONS, WERE MOVING AWAY UNDER COVER FROM THE FORCES OF ROBERT E. LEE.

THIS WAS NO ORDINARY MOVE. THE ARMY OF THE POTOMAC WAS GOING TO CROSS THE JAMES RIVER. WAITING FOR THEM WAS A FLEET OF TUGBOATS, FERRYBOATS, GUNBOATS, AND THE LONGEST PONTOON BRIDGE EVER BUILT: 2,100 FEET LONG.

IT WAS ONE OF THE MOST INCREDIBLE FEATS OF MILITARY ENGINEERING UP TO THAT TIME.

THE OBJECTIVE WAS PETERSBURG, 23 MILES SOUTH OF RICHMOND. PETERSBURG WAS THE TRANSPORATION HUB FOR RAIL LINES ENTERING AND LEAVING THE THE CONFEDERATE CAPITAL. IF IT FELL INTO UNION HANDS, BOTH RICHMOND'S AND LEE'S ARMY WOULD BE WITHOUT FOOD AND THE CONFEDERACY'S ABILITY TO SUSTAIN THE WAR WOULD BE SEVERELY HAMPERED. TROOPS FROM BUTLER'S ARMY OF THE JAMES WERE ORDERED TO ATTACK PETERSBURG ON JUNE 9, BUT, AS GRANT PUT IT, "THEIR CONDUCT . . . WAS TOO FEEBLE TO BE CALLED AN ATTACK." THE JOB WOULD NOW BE THE PRIORITY OF THE ARMY OF THE POTOMAC.

PART OF GRANT'S PLAN WAS FOR WILLIAM F. "BALDY" SMITH'S XVIII CORPS, WITH 16,000 MEN, TO CROSS THE JAMES AND ADVANCE ON PETERSBURG ALONG THE CITY POINT RAILROAD. HANCOCK'S II CORPS, WITH 22,000 MEN, WOULD CROSS AT WINDMILL POINT AND MARCH WEST TO JOIN THEM.

P. G. T. BEAUREGARD, WHO COMMANDED THE DEFENSE OF PETERSBURG, HAD ONLY 2,200 MEN IN THE DIMMOCK LINE, AN IMPRESSIVE STRING OF FORTIFICATIONS THAT FACED THE DIRECTION THAT SMITH AND HANCOCK WERE ARRIVING FROM.

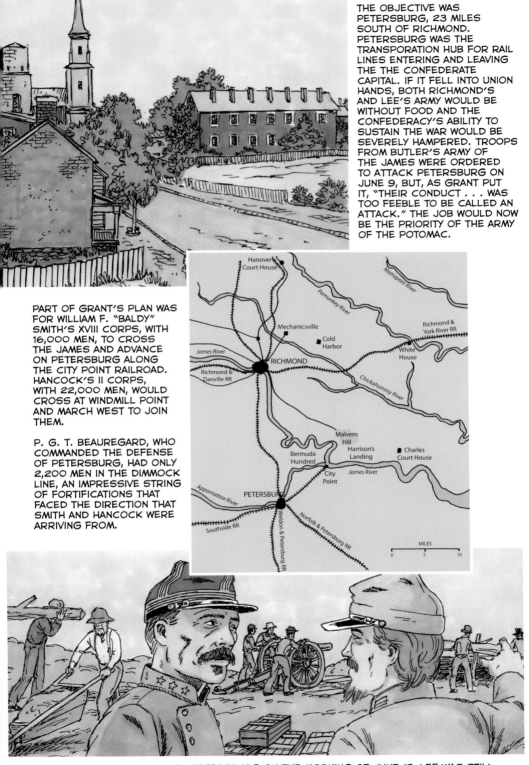

AS SMITH'S FORCES APPROACHED PETERSBURG ON THE MORNING OF JUNE 15, LEE WAS STILL UNAWARE THAT GRANT HAD PULLED HIS ARMY OUT OF COLD HARBOR.

AT 9AM, SMITH'S FORCES BEGAN A WEAK ASSAULT ON THE DIMMOCK LINE. SMITH'S CORPS FOUGHT AT COLD HARBOR, SO HE KNEW WHAT IT WAS LIKE TO ATTACK WELL-MANNED FORTIFICATIONS ACROSS OPEN GROUND.

FINALLY, AT 7 PM, SMITH DECIDED TO MAKE A MOVE. HE SENT HIS CORPS AGAINST THE NORTHERNMOST POINT OF THE FORTIFICATIONS.

IN THE LEFT WING OF SMITH'S ATTACK WAS THE BLACK DIVISION OF EDWARD W. HINKS. HE SENT HIS BATTLE-UNTESTED TROOPS FORWARD AT A RUN.

WITH GREAT SKILL AND JUBILATION, THE BLACK INFANTRYMEN CAPTURED SEVEN GUNS AND THEIR CREWS. THE ROAD TO PETERSBURG WAS OPEN. BUT SMITH TOOK ONE LOOK AT THE FORTIFICATIONS, WHICH HAD BEEN UNDER CONSTRUCTION FOR NEARLY TWO YEARS, AND STOPPED. HE REPORTED THE NEXT DAY THAT HE "THOUGHT IT PRUDENT TO MAKE NO FARTHER ADVANCE."

THE CONFEDERATES BEHIND BEAUREGARD'S WORKS WERE NOW WORN OUT. IF THEY WEREN'T DEFENDING THEMSELVES AGAINST UNION ATTACKS, THEY WERE DIGGING NEW WORKS.

LEE, FINALLY CONVINCED THAT GRANT HAD MOVED HIS ARMY ACROSS THE JAMES, BEGAN MOVING HIS FORCES SOUTH AT 3 AM ON JUNE 18.

LATER THAT MORNING, TWO OF LEE'S DIVISIONS FILED IN BEHIND BEAUREGARD'S TRENCHES. THE DEFENDERS OF PETERSBURG CHEERED AND WEPT WITH JOY.

BEAUREGARD NOW HAD 20,000 MEN UNDER HIS COMMAND, BUT GRANT HAD 67,000 PRESENT, AND THEY WERE ABOUT TO ATTACK.

JUNE 18 WOULD BE A BITTER DAY FOR THE ARMY OF THE POTOMAC. THE II CORPS BEGAN THE ATTACK EARLY THAT DAY AND AT NOON THE IX AND V CORPS JOINED IN. "I SHALL NEVER FORGET THE HURRICANE OF SHOT AND SHELL WHICH STRUCK US AS WE EMERGED FROM THE TREES," A CAPTAIN FROM THE 4TH NEW YORK HEAVY ARTILLERY REMEMBERED.

COLONEL JOSHUA LAWRENCE CHAMBERLAIN, WHO WON THE MEDAL OF HONOR FOR HIS ACTIONS AT THE BATTLE OF GETTYSBURG, LEAD HIS BRIGADE AGAINST RIVES' SALIENT WHEN HIS COLOR BEARER WAS KILLED.

CHAMBERLAIN SEIZED THE FLAG, BUT WAS IMMEDIATELY SHOT THROUGH BOTH HIPS. FOR WEEKS HE LAY IN AGONY AND WAS NOT EXPECTED TO LIVE.

ALL THE UNION ASSAULTS HAD FAILED, BUT MEADE ORDERED ANOTHER. IN THE VANGUARD OF THE UNION ATTACK WERE THE 900 MEN OF THE 1ST MAINE HEAVY ARTILLERY. THIS REGIMENT JUST RECENTLY ARRIVED FROM DEFENDING WASHINGTON, D.C., AND WERE NOW INFANTRY. THEY ADVANCED "LIKE A BLUE WAVE CRESTED WITH A GLISTENING FOAM OF STEEL."

WITHIN A FEW MINUTES THEY WERE IN RANGE OF THE CONFEDERATE WORKS, AND THE FIRE TORE THEM TO PIECES. 632 OF THEIR MEN FELL, THE HEAVIEST BATTLE LOSS OF ANY REGIMENT DURING THE ENTIRE WAR.

GRANT DID NOT WANT ANOTHER SIEGE LIKE VICKSBURG, BUT HE HAD TO FORCE LEE OUT INTO THE OPEN AND HE AIMED TO DO THIS BY SENDING THE CAVALRY DIVISIONS OF JAMES H. WILSON AND AUGUST V. KAUTZ OUT TO CUT THE LAST TWO RAIL LINES THAT SUPPLIED LEE'S ARMY: THE WELDON AND SOUTHSIDE RAILROADS. BEFORE DAWN ON JUNE 22, NEARLY 5,000 TROOPERS SET OUT TO TEAR UP THE TWO RAILROADS.

LIKE MANY CAVALRY RAIDS DURING THE WAR, THIS RAID YIELDED MIXED RESULTS. THEY DESTROYED NEARLY 60 MILES OF TRACK AND HINDERED LEE'S SUPPLY SITUATION, BUT THIS DIDN'T FORCE THE REBELS OUT OF PETERSBURG, MUCH LESS RICHMOND. THE UNION SOLDIERS LOST ALL THEIR ARTILLERY, WAGONS, SUPPLIES, AND A QUARTER OF THEIR MEN.

NEITHER GRANT NOR LEE WANTED A SIEGE, BUT THAT IS EXACTLY WHAT WAS SHAPING UP AROUND PETERSBURG. SOMETHING DRASTIC, OR MAYBE EVEN CRAZY, WAS GOING TO HAVE TO HAPPEN TO BREAK THIS SIEGE.

THE CRATER JUNE 1864

AT PETERSBURG, MAJ. GEN. AMBROSE BURNSIDE'S CORPS HELD THE CENTER OF THE FEDERAL LINE.

ONE OF THESE REGIMENTS WAS THE 48TH PENNSYLVANIA, WHOSE MEN HAD WORKED AS ANTHRACITE MINERS IN SCHUYLKILL COUNTY. THESE WERE HARD-WORKING MEN, AND THE IDLE LIFE OF TRENCH WARFARE DID NOT APPEAL TO THEM AT ALL.

THE 48TH'S COMMANDER, HENRY PLEASANTS, CAME UP WITH A NOVEL IDEA ON HOW TO KEEP HIS MEN BUSY AND ADVANCE THROUGH THE CONFEDERATE'S EARTHWORKS AS WELL: DIG UNDER THEM.

THE MINERS WOULD DIG A 500-FOOT TUNNEL, COMPLETE WITH VENTILATION SHAFT, UNDER THE CONFEDERATE WORKS CALLED ELLIOTT'S SALIENT. THEY WOULD THEN DIG TWO LATERAL TUNNELS UNDER THE REBEL TRENCHES, FILL THEM WITH GUNPOWDER, AND IGNITE THEM PRIOR TO AN INFANTRY ASSAULT.

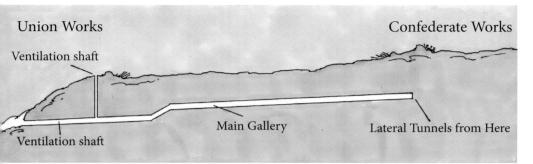

Union Works

Confederate Works

Ventilation shaft

Main Gallery

Lateral Tunnels from Here

Ventilation shaft

NEITHER GRANT NOR MEADE TOOK MUCH INTEREST IN THE TUNNEL DIGGING AND CONSIDERED IT A DIVERSION TO KEEP MEN OCCUPIED DURING A LULL IN THE FIGHTING.

BECAUSE OF THIS, BURNSIDE AND PLEASANTS CONCEIVED OF AND WORKED ON THIS PLAN ON THEIR OWN, RECEIVING LITTLE AID OR SUPPORT.

IT DIDN'T TAKE LONG BEFORE THE CONFEDERATES GREW SUSPICIOUS. ORDINANCE CHIEF BRIG. GEN. E. PORTER ALEXANDER WAS THE FIRST TO SUSPECT SOMETHING BECAUSE OF THE LARGE NUMBER OF FEDERAL SHARPSHOOTERS IN THE AREA.

OTHERS IN THE CONFEDERATE WORKS THOUGHT THEY HEARD SUSPICIOUS SOUNDS COMING FROM THE EARTH, BUT FEW TOOK IT SERIOUSLY.

THE MINERS CONTINUED TO DIG. THE TUNNEL WAS FIVE FEET HIGH, FOUR FEET WIDE AT THE BOTTOM AND TWO FEET WIDE AT THE TOP. THREE MEN WOULD WORK AT A TIME, ONE DIGGING AND THE TWO OTHERS REMOVING THE DIRT. THEY MADE PROGRESS OF 40 FEET A DAY.

ONCE THE TUNNEL WAS FINISHED, THE UNION OFFICERS FINALLY SHOWED INTEREST AND ORDERED THE MINERS TO FILL THE SOUTHERN END OF THE TUNNEL WITH 320 KEGS OF BLACK POWDER.

THE ASSAULT TROOPS WERE MOVED TO THE FRONT. THE EXPLOSION WAS PLANNED TO IGNITE AT DAWN, SATURDAY, JULY 30.

THE 98-FOOT FUSE WAS LIT AT 4:15 AM.

THE UNION TROOPS WAITED, WAITED . . . WAITED . . .

MEANWHILE, SEVERAL REGIMENTS OF FEDERAL BLACK TROOPS HAD ADVANCED BEYOND THEIR TRENCHES TO THE EDGE OF THE CRATER.

THEY SOMEHOW MANAGED TO GET THROUGH THE MASS OF MEN, CRAWL UP THE FAR BANK, AND FORM ON THE OTHER SIDE.

THEY BEGAN THEIR TO ADVANCE TOWARD PETERSBURG.

THESE FEDERALS AND CONFEDERATES COLLIDED AND THE FEDERALS WERE HEAVILY OUTNUMBERED. WHEN THE REBELS SAW THAT THEY WERE FIGHTING BLACK TROOPS, THEY WERE SHOCKED, STARTLED, AND ENRAGED.

THE CONFEDERATES PUSHED BACK THE FEDERAL LINE, MOST OF THE TIME NOT ACCEPTING THE SURRENDER OF THE BLACK TROOPS. THEY SHOUTED, "TAKE THE OFFICERS! KILL THE NIGGERS."

THE CONFEDERATES ADVANCED TO THE EDGE OF THE CRATER AND BEGAN FIRING DOWN INTO IT.

"THE SLAUGHTER WAS FEARFUL," ONE OF MAHONE'S OFFICERS RECALLED. MANY MEN IN THE CRATER TRIED TO FIGHT BACK; OTHERS SURRENDERED. OTHERS MERELY TRIED TO FLEE. IT DIDN'T MATTER. THEY WERE SITTING DUCKS IN THE CRATER.

BY 2 PM IT WAS ALL OVER. THE CONFEDERATES ESTABLISHED A NEW TRENCH LINE IN FRONT OF THE CRATER. THE FEDERALS LOST 3,500 KILLED, WOUNDED, AND MISSING. THE CONFEDERATES LOST ABOUT 1,500.

"IT WAS THE SADDEST AFFAIR I HAVE WITNESSED IN THE WAR," GRANT WIRED TO WASHINGTON, D.C. THE NEXT DAY. GENERAL BURNSIDE WAS SENT HOME ON LEAVE AND NEVER RECALLED TO DUTY.

THE BEEFSTEAK RAID AUGUST 1864

WINFIELD SCOTT HANCOCK, COMMANDER OF THE FEDERAL II CORPS, WAS SUFFERING FROM HIS OLD WOUND THAT HE RECEIVED AT GETTYSBURG MORE THAN A YEAR EARLIER.

FRANCIS BARLOW, WHO COMMANDED SCOTT'S 1ST DIVISION, WAS ALSO SUFFERING FROM OLD WOUNDS FROM THE BATTLE AT GETTYSBURG, WHERE HE HAD BEEN LEFT ON THE FIELD OF BATTLE FOR DEAD.

CONFEDERATE GEN. JOHN B. GORDON FOUND HIM AND TENDED AND ARRANGED TO GET HIM IN THE CARE OF MRS. BARLOW, WHO WAS A FEDERAL ARMY NURSE. GORDON WAS SYMPATHETIC. HE HIMSELF HAD BEEN SHOT FIVE TIMES AT ANTIETAM.

JOHN B. GORDON WAS NOW AMONG THE CONFEDERATE TROOPS FACING BARLOW ACROSS THE TRENCHES AT PETERSBURG.

THE ARMY OF THE POTOMAC WAS IN BAD SHAPE, TOO. BY EARLY AUGUST, HIGH CASUALTIES AND EXPIRED ENLISTMENTS REDUCED THE SIZE OF THE ARMY CONSIDERABLY. THE FEDERAL REPLACEMENT SYSTEM DID NOT HELP.

THESE REPLACEMENTS WEREN'T EXCEPTIONAL SOLDIERS: THEY WERE SULLEN DRAFTEES, PAID SUBSTITUTES, AND BOUNTY JUMPERS, POORLY TRAINED AND POORLY MOTIVATED.

THE CONFEDERATES, OF COURSE, WERE IN MUCH WORSE SHAPE, BUT THEY SOMEHOW SEEMED TO MOVE FORWARD. THERE WERE NO REPLACEMENTS FOR THEM AND THEIR RATIONS CONTINUED TO BE MEAGER: RANCID BACON AND UNCOOKED CORNMEAL. THEIR CLOTHING WAS TATTERED AND IN RAGS.

ON AUGUST 25, CONFEDERATE TROOPS OF A. P. HILL ATTACKED HANCOCK'S II CORPS AT REAM'S STATION.

THREE GREEN NEW YORK REGIMENTS, WHICH WERE RECENTLY ASSIGNED TO JOHN GIBBON'S DIVISION, SIMPLY CAVED IN. MANY FLED, BUT MOST SURRENDERED, PREFERRING PRISON TO COMBAT.

A GREEN RESERVE BRIGADE REFUSED TO MOVE FORWARD TO FILL THE GAP.

HANCOCK RODE FORWARD AND TRIED TO RALLY HIS MEN, CALLING, "WE CAN BEAT THEM YET! DON'T LEAVE ME, FOR GOD'S SAKE!"

HIS CORPS LOST 2,750 KILLED, WOUNDED, OR MISSING. NINE CANNONS, A DOZEN BATTLE FLAGS, AND WELL OVER 3,000 RIFLES LAY ABANDONED ON THE FIELD. THE CONFEDERATE LOSSES WERE ABOUT 720.

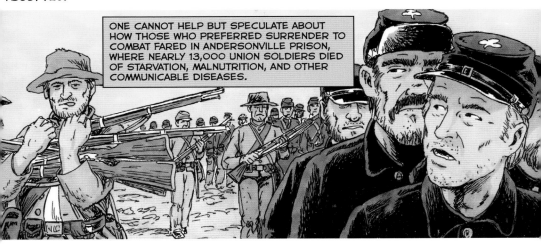

ONE CANNOT HELP BUT SPECULATE ABOUT HOW THOSE WHO PREFERRED SURRENDER TO COMBAT FARED IN ANDERSONVILLE PRISON, WHERE NEARLY 13,000 UNION SOLDIERS DIED OF STARVATION, MALNUTRITION, AND OTHER COMMUNICABLE DISEASES.

SERGEANT GEORGE SHADBURNE WAS A CONFEDERATE SCOUT FOR CAVALRY GEN. WADE HAMPTON AND HAD CAMPED TWO MILES BEHIND THE UNION LINES NEAR CITY POINT ON THE JAMES RIVER, THE FEDERAL SUPPLY BASE. HE DELIVERED A MESSAGE TO HAMPTON:

"AT COGGINS' POINT ARE 3,000 BEEVES, ATTENDED BY 120 MEN, AND 30 CITIZENS WITHOUT ARMS."

HAMPTON WAS INTRIGUED. THE CONFEDERACY WAS DESPERATELY SHORT OF SUPPLIES AND THOSE 3,000 CATTLE WOULD FEED THE FORCES AROUND PETERSBURG FOR NEARLY SIX WEEKS.

SHADBURNE ALSO FOUND OUT THAT GRANT WOULD BE GOING TO THE SHENANDOAH VALLEY TO MEET WITH SHERIDAN TO DISCUSS UPCOMING PLANS ON SEPTEMBER 14. HAMPTON FELT A RAID WOULD HAVE A BETTER CHANCE OF SUCCESS IF GRANT WAS GONE.

HAMPTON AND 4,500 TROOPERS LEFT THE CONFEDERATE LINE SOUTH OF PETERSBURG ON SEPTEMBER 14. SERGEANT SHADBURNE WAS IN THE LEAD. THEY TURNED NORTHEAST WHERE THEY HAD TO REBUILD COOK'S BRIDGE OVER THE BLACKWATER RIVER THE FIRST NIGHT.

THE NEXT DAY, AS THEY RODE NORTH, GEN. ROONEY LEE (THE ARMY COMMANDER'S SON) TOOK HIS DIVISION TO THE LEFT. HE WAS ORDERED TO STAY BETWEEN THE CATTLE HERD AND THE FEDERAL FORCES AS LONG AS POSSIBLE.

BRIGADIER GENERAL JAMES DEARING'S BRIGADE MOVED RIGHT TO PROTECT THEIR FLANK.

EARLY THE NEXT MORNING, AFTER A SMALL FIGHT WITH THE 1ST D.C. AND 13TH PENNSYLVANIA CAVALRIES, HAMPTON AND HIS MEN CAPTURED THE HERD.

ON THE MORNING OF SEPTEMBER 16, THEY DROVE THE CATTLE INTO THE CONFEDERATE LINES WITH THE COST OF 10 DEAD AND 47 WOUNDED. WHAT WAS THE FINAL TALLY? HAMPTON AND HIS MEN DELIVERED 2,468 STEERS, 11 WAGONS FILLED WITH SUPPLIES, AND 304 PRISONERS.

THAT NIGHT THE CONFEDERATES DINED LAVISHLY, AND THERE WAS PLENTY FOR EVERYBODY FOR THE FIRST TIME IN A LONG WHILE.

FOR THE NEXT SEVERAL WEEKS, THE REBS WOULD STAND ON THEIR BREASTWORKS AND CALL OUT, "GOOD FAT BEEF OVER HERE! COME OVER AND GET SOME!" AND RATHER THAN CALL THE REBEL YELL, THEY WOULD GLEEFULLY BELLOW LIKE BULLS.

STALEMATE SEPTEMBER 1864

BY SEPTEMBER 1864, BOTH ARMIES HAD EXHAUSTED THEMSELVES AND AN UNEASY LULL SETTLED ACROSS THE BATTLEFIELD. THE ONLY MILITARY ACTION WAS ONE SIDE OR THE OTHER FIRING A FEW SHELLS OR SHARPSHOOTERS TRYING TO PICK OFF SOME ILL-ADVISED JOHNNY OR BILLY WHO WAS DUMB OR UNLUCKY ENOUGH TO STICK HIS HEAD UP.

THERE WAS GOOD NEWS FOR THE UNION, HOWEVER. SHERMAN HAD TAKEN ATLANTA AND PHIL SHERIDAN DEFEATED JUBAL EARLY IN THE SHENANDOAH.

FOR THE REBELS, THERE WAS NOTHING BUT BAD NEWS: MANY A STEADFAST VETERAN, WORRYING ABOUT HIS FAMILY AT HOME, DECIDED IT WAS TIME TO IT QUIT.

THE FEDERAL FORCES WEREN'T IDLE FOR LONG. THEIR NEXT ATTACK WOULD BE NORTH OF THE JAMES RIVER IN THE AREA OCCUPIED BY BEN BUTLER'S ARMY OF THE JAMES. BUTLER PROPOSED A THREE-PRONGED ATTACK AGAINST THE CONFEDERATE DEFENSES AT NEW MARKET AND CHAFFIN'S BLUFF.

GRANT HOPED THAT THIS WOULD DRAW CONFEDERATE FORCES NORTH OF THE RIVER AND WEAKEN THEIR HOLD ON THE SOUTHSIDE RAILROAD.

APPROXIMIATELY 18,000 FEDERAL TROOPS WOULD TAKE PART IN THE ASSAULT, INCLUDING SEVERAL REGIMENTS OF BLACK TROOPS. THE ADVANCE BEGAN AT 4:30 AM, SEPTEMBER 29. THE TANGLED AND SWAMPY COUNTRYSIDE MADE IT DIFFICULT TO FOR THE TROOPS TO MANEUVER AND MAINTAIN A UNIFIED FRONT.

THE CONFEDERATES BUILT AN ELABORATE TRIPLE-LINE OF EARTHWORKS BETWEEN BUTLER'S ARMY AND RICHMOND. THEIR PROBLEM WAS MANPOWER: THEY HAD ONLY 4,000 TROOPS TO MAN THEM. THE CONFEDERATES HAD TO SHIFT AROUND IN THE WORKS AND GUESS WHERE THE YANKEES WOULD HIT. FORTUNATELY FOR THEM, ON THE MORNING OF THE ATTACK, THEY WERE AT THE RIGHT PLACE AT THE RIGHT TIME.

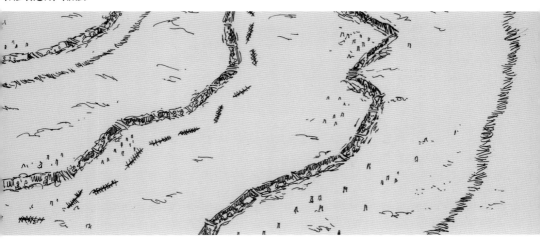

THE FEDERAL TROOPS HIT THE CONFEDERATE WORKS IN A THICK FOG. IN THE FIRST ATTACK, THE 6TH US COLORED TROOPS WERE "CUT TO PIECES." THEY FELL BACK AND REGROUPED AND CHARGED THE WORKS AGAIN, ONLY TO FIND THEM ABANDONED. THE REBELS HAD FALLEN BACK TO DEFEND FORT HARRISON.

MAJOR GENERAL EDWARD ORD'S 8,000 MEN ADVANCED WITHIN A FEW MILES OF THE FORT. THEY WOULD HAVE TO ADVANCE A MILE OVER CLEARED, RISING GROUND WITHIN SIGHT OF THE ENEMY'S GUNS AND MUSKETS. ORD, WHO IN HIS LONG MILITARY CAREER HAD NEVER LED SUCH AN ASSAULT, WAS RELUCTANT TO MOVE. FINALLY, AFTER THE URGING OF SUBORDINATES, HE GAVE THE ORDER FOR THE ADVANCE TO BEGIN.

ORD DIDN'T KNOW IT, BUT THE FORT WAS DEFENDED BY ONLY 800 INEXPERIENCED MEN OF THE HEAVY ARTILLERY, SEVERAL OF WHOM FOUND OUT THAT THEIR GUNS WEREN'T WORKING.

AS THE FEDERAL FORCES ADVANCED WITHIN A FEW YARDS OF FORT HARRISON, THE CONFEDERATE DEFENDERS REALIZED THAT THEIR CANNON COULD NOT POINT DOWN ENOUGH TO FIRE ON THE ENEMY. WHEN THE YANKEES CAME SPILLING OVER THE BREASTWORKS AND ALSO THROUGH THE GUN APERTURES, THE REBELS BROKE AND RAN.

NOW BUTLER WAS ONLY ABOUT FIVE MILES FROM RICHMOND, BUT HE WAS STARTING TO LOSE CONTROL OF HIS TROOPS.

NOT WANTING TO LOSE THE INITIATIVE, ORD GATHERED WHAT MEN HE COULD FROM NEARBY AND BEGAN TO ADVANCE AGAINST THE CONFEDERATE TRENCHES.

CONFEDERATE ARTILLERYMEN IN FORT HOKE GRABBED SMOOTH-BORE MUSKETS AND FOUGHT BACK, BREAKING UP ORD'S ATTACK AND WOUNDING THE GENERAL IN THE LEG, PUTTING HIM OUT OF ACTION.

THE GUNNERS AT FORT HOKE RECEIVED HELP FROM AN UNEXPECTED SOURCE. TWO CONFEDERATE IRONCLADS, THE *FREDERICKSBURG* AND THE *RICHMOND*, JUST HAPPENED TO BE COMING DOWN THE RIVER, SAW THE FEDERAL ATTACK, AND JOINED IN THE FIGHT.

TWO THINGS HAPPENED FOR THE CONFEDERATES. ONE-LEGGED DICK EWELL, WHO HAD BEEN RELIEVED BY LEE EARLIER DUE TO ILLNESS, ROSE TO THE OCCASION. HE TOOK PERSONAL CHARGE OF THE DEFENDERS OF CHAFFIN'S BLUFF.

BY NOON, LEE ORDERED REINFORCEMENTS TO CHAFFIN'S BLUFF. THE CONFEDERATE DEFENSES BEGAN TO TIGHTEN.

BY MIDAFTERNOON, THE FEDERALS REALIZED
THAT CONFEDERATE REINFORCEMENTS WERE
POURING INTO THE TRENCHES IN FRONT OF
THEM. THEY REALIZED THE DANGER AND BEGAN
TO DIG IN. SOME OF THEIR UNITS SUFFERED 35
PERCENT CASUALTIES.

ALL NIGHT LONG MORE AND MORE
CONFEDERATES FILTERED INTO THE LINE. BY THE
NEXT MORNING THERE WERE 16,000 OF THEM.

THE NEXT AFTERNOON, LEE SENT THEM TO RECAPTURE FORT HARRISON. THE FEDERALS WERE
READY FOR THEM.

THE CONFEDERATES WERE CUT DOWN IN A HAIL OF FIRE. 1,200 FELL, AND FORT HARRISON WAS
STILL IN UNION HANDS.

TO GENERAL LEE THE VERY IDEA OF LEAVING FORT HARRISON IN UNION HANDS WAS INTOLERABLE,
BUT FOR THE TIME BEING THERE WASN'T ANYTHING HE COULD DO.

ON THE SAME DAY, SEPTEMBER 30, FOUR UNION DIVISIONS MOVED BELOW THE SOUTHERNMOST LINE BELOW PETERSBURG, TRYING TO FLANK THE REBEL LINE AND CUT THE SOUTH SIDE RAILROAD.

WHEN THE CONFEDERATES COUNTERATTACKED, THE UNION ASSAULT FELL APART AND MANY FEDERAL SOLDIERS STAMPEDED TOWARD THE REAR. THE REBELS TOOK A STAGGERING 1,300 PRISONERS.

THE CONFEDERATE ATTACK WAS FINALLY STOPPED WHEN COL. JOSEPH GRIFFIN PLACED CANNONS RIGHT IN LINE WITH HIS INFANTRY.

IN OCTOBER, LEE TRIED TO RETAKE FORT HARRISON AND GRANT AGAIN TRIED TO CUT THE SOUTH SIDE RAILROAD. NEITHER SUCCEEDED AND ONLY THE CASUALTIES GREW.

"WE MAY BE ABLE, WITH THE BLESSING OF GOD, TO KEEP THE ENEMY IN CHECK UNTIL THE BEGINNING OF WINTER," LEE WROTE. "IF WE FAIL TO DO THIS THE RESULT MAY BE CALAMITOUS."

THE AUTUMN RAINS SET IN AND DOWNPOURS SOMETIMES LASTED FOR DAYS. IN A SENSE, LEE HAD WON A LIMITED VICTORY. HE ACHIEVED HIS GOAL OF HOLDING OUT UNTIL WINTER.

NOVEMBER 8, ABRAHAM LINCOLN WAS ELECTED TO A SECOND TERM AS US PRESIDENT BY A HUGE MAJORITY.

BY NOW THE UNION RAILROAD RAN FROM THEIR SUPPLY CENTER AT CITY POINT, RIGHT UP TO THE FRONT LINES. THE AVERAGE YANKEE COULD ENJOY ALL THE BENEFITS OF HIS NATION'S ABUNDANCE. PRESIDENT LINCOLN DECLARED THE LAST THURSDAY OF NOVEMBER AS THANKSGIVING DAY. THE NOW 120,000 SOLDIERS OF THE ARMY OF THE POTOMAC AND ARMY OF THE JAMES ENJOYED TURKEY OR CHICKEN, PIES, AND FRUIT.

IN THE TRENCHES FACING THEM, THE 57,000 MEN OF THE ARMY OF NORTHERN VIRGINIA ATE THEIR STANDARD MEAL OF RANCID BACON AND RAW CORNMEAL. THEY DID, HOWEVER, HOLD THEIR FIRE IN HONOR OF THE UNION HOLIDAY.

A SOUTH CAROLINA CAPTAIN WROTE: "THE CONVICTION EVERYWHERE PREVAILED THAT WE COULD SUSTAIN BUT ONE MORE CAMPAIGN."

FORT STEDMAN WINTER 1864–1865

THROUGHOUT THE WINTER OF 1864–1865, ONE SUBJECT DOMINATED THE THOUGHTS OF EVERYONE IN THE ARMY OF NORTHERN VIRGINIA, FROM LEE RIGHT DOWN TO THE LOWEST PRIVATE: FOOD!– OR RATHER, THE LACK OF IT. THE SOLDIERS KNEW THEY WERE NOT THE ONLY ONES SUFFERING. WHEN THE WOMEN OF RICHMOND ANNOUNCED THEY WERE PREPARING A NEW YEAR'S DAY FEAST FOR THE ARMY, ALL THE MEN WERE EXCITED. UNFORTUNATELY, ALL THE WOMEN WERE ABLE TO SERVE WAS A SINGLE HAM AND BISCUIT FOR EACH MAN.

EVERYONE SUFFERED ALIKE. WHEN AN IRISH MEMBER OF PARLIAMENT VISITED GENERAL LEE, HE WAS INVITED TO DINNER. ALL LEE HAD TO EAT WAS TWO BISCUITS, AND HE GAVE ONE TO HIS GUEST.

FRATERNIZATION WAS ALSO A PROBLEM. MEN FROM BOTH SIDES WOULD MEET BETWEEN THE LINES TO TRADE GOODS. THE UNION SOLDIERS ALWAYS HAD MORE PROVISIONS, SO THE TRADING WAS MORE FOR THE SOUTHERNERS' ADVANTAGE.

GENERALS GORDON AND ORD MET TO DISCUSS THIS ISSUE AND THEIR DISCUSSION BECAME ONE ON THE NEED FOR PEACE, SO, IN A SENSE, THEY WERE ALSO FRATERNIZING.

PRESIDENT LINCOLN RELUCTANTLY SENT OUT PROPOSALS FOR DISCUSSING A PEACE TREATY AND PRESIDENT DAVIS SENT A COMMISSION TO MEET. THESE TALKS, HOWEVER, ALWAYS STALLED ON LINCOLN'S TWO PRIMARY DEMANDS: RESTORATIONS OF THE UNION AND THE ABOLITION OF SLAVERY.

IT WAS CLEAR TO BOTH SIDES THAT THE WAR WOULD HAVE TO BE FOUGHT TO A CONCLUSION.

BETWEEN FEBRUARY 5 AND 7, GRANT AGAIN SENT HIS FORCES SOUTH, TRYING TO FLANK THE CONFEDERATE LINE BELOW PETERSBURG. THE FIGHT AT HATCHER'S RUN CAUSED LEE TO EXTEND HIS LINE TO 37 MILES OF FORTIFICATIONS. NOW, WITH ONLY ABOUT 50,000 MEN, HE WAS STRETCHED AND WOULD SOON BE UNABLE TO HOLD THE LINE.

LEE KNEW HE HAD TO DO WHAT HE HAD FREQUENTLY DONE DURING THREE YEARS OF WAR: ATTACK! HE WOULD HAVE TO BREAK OUT OF THE PETERSBURG TRAP, LEAVING RICHMOND TO THE ENEMY.

BUT WHERE COULD HE BREAK OUT? LEE GAVE THE JOB OF STUDYING THE PROBLEM TO HIS YOUNGEST CORPS COMMANDER, JOHN B. GORDON.

PERHAPS THEY COULD MOVE SOUTH AND JOIN JOE JOHNSTON'S ARMY OF TENNESSEE, WHO WERE NOW FIGHTING GENERAL SHERMAN IN THE CAROLINAS.

GORDON STUDIED THE PROBLEM FOR THREE WEEKS BEFORE HE CAME BACK TO GENERAL LEE WITH A PROPOSAL. HE FELT THE BEST PLACE TO ATTACK WAS THE FEDERAL STRONGPOINT OF FORT STEDMAN. FORT STEDMAN WAS ONLY 150 YARDS FROM THE CONFEDERATE TRENCHES. IT WAS A STRONG POSITION, BUT GORDON'S UNORTHODOX PLAN HAD PROMISE.

AT 4 AM ON THE MORNING OF MARCH 25, A GROUP OF MEN FROM THE 57TH NORTH CAROLINA REGIMENT SLIPPED SILENTLY ACROSS THE LINES TOWARD FORT STEDMAN. THEY WERE ARMED ONLY WITH AXES.

A SHOT RANG OUT! THEY HAD BEEN SPOTTED BY A FEDERAL PICKET. WITHOUT HESITATION, THE MEN TORE INTO THE BARRIERS AND SPUN THE CHEVAUX-DE-FRISE OUT OF THE WAY.

TWO MORE CONFEDERATE REGIMENTS WERE RIGHT ON THEIR HEELS.

FORT STEDMAN'S DEFENDERS WERE COMPLETELY TAKEN BY SURPRISE AND QUICKLY OVERPOWERED. THE CONFEDERATES TOOK MANY PRISONERS.

A SELECT TEAM OF ARTILLERISTS QUICKLY TOOK OVER THE FORT'S GUNS.

THEY TURNED THESE GUNS ON UNION POSITIONS BOTH NORTH AND SOUTH OF THEIR POSITION AND BEGAN FIRING ON THEM.

THE CONFEDERATES THEN BEGAN PRESSING NORTH WITH THE INTENTION OF ROLLING UP THE UNION LINE. THEY STRUCK THE 57TH MASSACHUSETTS, WHO WERE UNPREPARED, AND TOOK MORE PRISONERS.

AS THE CONFEDERATES PUSHED FARTHER NORTH, THEY FOUND THAT THE FEDERALS WERE WAKING UP. THE DEFENDERS OF BATTERY #9 WERE DETERMINED TO MAKE A STAND AND DROVE THE ATTACKERS TO THE GROUND.

THE CONFEDERATES TURNED TOWARD FORT HASKELL, WHICH WAS LOCATED SOUTH OF FORT STEDMAN. UNION GUNNERS TURNED THREE OF THEIR NAPOLEONS ON THE REBELS AND BLASTED THEM WITH DEADLY CANISTER FIRE.

AS DAYLIGHT ARRIVED, FEDERAL FORCES WERE NOW REACTING MORE CONSISTENTLY AND QUICKLY MOVING MORE AND MORE TROOPS TO THE TRENCHES AROUND FORT STEDMAN.

MEANWHILE, THE CONFEDERATES IN FORT STEDMAN WERE HAVING A QUICK FEAST ON THE FEDERAL RATIONS THEY FOUND.

BY 8 AM THE LANDSCAPE AROUND FORT STEDMAN WAS COVERED WITH FEDERAL TROOPS. GENERAL LEE SENT WORD TO GORDON FOR HIS FORCES TO WITHDRAW.

THE UNION FIRE WAS HAZARDOUS FOR THE CONFEDERATES ATTEMPTING TO REACH THEIR OWN LINES AND MANY WERE CUT DOWN TRYING TO MAKE IT BACK. HUNDREDS OF OTHERS JUST STAYED IN FORT STEDMAN AND WERE CAPTURED.

THE CONFEDERATE LOSS WAS 1,600 KILLED AND WOUNDED AND 1,900 CAPTURED. THE FEDERALS LOST ABOUT 1,000, HALF OF THEM PRISONERS. IT WAS CLEAR TO LEE HOW EASY THE NORTHERNERS HAD STOPPED THE ASSAULT. THE DAY AFTER THE FORT STEDMAN ATTACK, HE INFORMED PRESIDENT DAVIS THAT HIS POSITION AT PETERSBURG WAS DOOMED. HE WOULD NOW HAVE TO FIND A WAY TO WITHDRAW HIS REMAINING MEN TO THE SOUTHEAST WITHOUT A GENERAL ENGAGEMENT AGAINST GRANT'S SUPERIOR FORCES.

THE FIVE FORKS

GRANT ANTICIPATED LEE'S MOVE TO DISENGAGE AT PETERSBURG AND TO MOVE SOUTH TO LINK UP WITH JOE JOHNSTON. HE PLANNED TO PREVENT IT AND WOULD MOVE THE MEN OF THE V CORPS SOUTH AND WEST TO BLOCK LEE'S ARMY AT A CROSSROADS CALLED FIVE FORKS. HE WOULD ALSO SEND PHIL SHERIDAN WITH 11,000 CAVALRYMEN, MOST OF WHOM HAD JUST RETURNED FROM THEIR VICTORY OVER JUBAL EARLY.

ON THE MORNING OF WEDNESDAY, MARCH 29, LEE LEARNED ABOUT THESE MOVEMENTS AND IMMEDIATELY UNDERSTOOD GRANT'S INTENTIONS. HE DECIDED TO SEND GEORGE PICKETT'S DIVISION TO FIVE FORKS. HE ALSO SENT 5,500 CAVALRYMEN UNDER FITZHUGH LEE (HIS NEPHEW) AND ROONEY LEE (HIS SON).

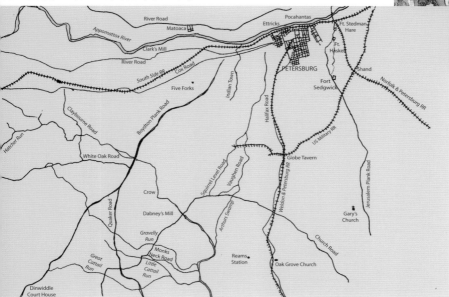

ON THAT SAME DAY, THE LEAD ELEMENT OF WARREN'S V CORPS APPROACHED A SAWMILL NEAR GRAVELLY RUN WHEN IT ENCOUNTERED CONFEDERATE SKIRMISHERS. THE LEAD BRIGADE WAS COMMANDED BY JOSHUA LAWRENCE CHAMBERLAIN, WHO HAD RECOVERED FROM HIS BAD WOUND AND WAS NOW IN COMMAND AGAIN. DURING THIS FIGHT, A BULLET PASSED THROUGH CHAMBERLAIN'S HORSE'S NECK AND STRUCK HIM IN THE CHEST, DEFLECTING OFF A LEATHER-CASED MIRROR IN HIS POCKET.

CHAMBERLAIN WAS KNOCKED UNCONSCIOUS AND WHEN HE RECOVERED, HE FOUND HIS DIVISION COMMANDER, GEN. CHARLES GRIFFIN, STANDING OVER HIM.

CHAMBERLAIN GOT BACK ON HIS WOUNDED HORSE, IN WHICH HE NOW HAD "A BLOOD RELATIONSHIP OF WHICH I AM NOT ASHAMED."

CHAMBERLAIN RAILED HIS BRIGADE AND THEN DROVE OFF THE REBELS.

THAT AFTERNOON, UNION CAVALRY FOUND ELEMENTS OF PICKETT'S MEN ENTRENCHED AT FIVE FORKS. IT WAS CLEAR TO THEM THAT LEE HAD ANTICIPATED GRANT'S MOVE.

THE CONFEDERACY MAY HAVE BEEN ON THE OFFENSIVE, BUT ROBERT E. LEE HAD NOT CHANGED. WHILE PICKETT WAS FIGHTING SHERIDAN'S CAVALRY, HE WOULD ATTACK THE UNION INFANTRY.

LEE ALSO TOLD PICKETT TO SEND A LARGE FORCE AROUND SHERIDAN'S LEFT.

FOR THIS HE WOULD DRAW AND USE BRIGADES FROM A. P. HILL AND RICHARD ANDERSON.

BY THE MORNING OF MARCH 31, THE RAIN HAD STOPPED AND SHERIDAN WAS EAGER TO "GO TO SMASHING THINGS." AT 2 PM, HOWEVER, HE WAS HIT HARD BY PICKETT'S FLANKING FORCE AND ROONEY LEE'S CAVALRY. DESPITE SUPREME EFFORTS TO HOLD, THE CONFEDERATES DROVE THEM STEADILY SOUTHWARD.

SHERIDAN COOLY BROUGHT HIS CAVALRY UNITS TO FORM A LINE. GEORGE ARMSTRONG CUSTER'S DIVISION MANAGED TO FORM A LINE ON A SMALL RISE IN FRONT OF THE VILLAGE OF DINNWIDDIE AND WITHSTAND TWO ASSAULTS.

TO THE EAST, WARREN'S V CORPS HAD UNWITTINGLY MARCHED RIGHT INTO ANDERSON'S FLANKING ATTACK. SEVERAL OF THE BLUE DIVISIONS GAVE WAY IN THE FEROCIOUS ONSLAUGHT.

GRIFFIN'S DIVISION, HOWEVER, HELD ON. BY MIDAFTERNOON, JOSHUA CHAMBERLAIN'S BRIGADE WAS ORDERED TO COUNTERATTACK. "WILL YOU SAVE THE HONOR OF THE V CORPS?" WARREN ASKED IN AN EMOTIONAL VOICE. DESPITE THE PAIN OF HIS RECENT WOUND, CHAMBERLAIN LED AN ATTACK THAT DROVE BACK THE CONFEDERATES AND EVOKED ADMIRATION FROM BOTH SIDES.

SHERIDAN'S CAVALRY WAS ISOLATED, CUT OFF FROM THE ARMY OF THE POTOMAC. BUT HE REALIZED THAT IF IT WAS TRUE FOR HIM, IT WAS TRUE FOR THE REBS TOO.

GOUVERNEUR WARREN REALIZED THIS, TOO. HE KNEW PICKETT WAS VULNERABLE, AND HE PROPOSED TO GRANT THAT HE WOULD SEND GRIFFIN'S DIVISION TO SHERIDAN AND TAKE HIS OTHER TWO DIVISIONS AROUND TO THE ENEMY'S REAR.

GETTING HIS TWO DIVISIONS BEHIND PICKETT PROVED DIFFICULT. BRIDGES WERE DAMAGED AND HAD TO BE REPAIRED, AND ROADS WERE NEARLY WASHED OUT IN PLACES.

BY THE TIME WARREN HAD HIS TROOPS IN POSITION AT 7 AM, APRIL 1, PICKETT'S DIVISION WAS GONE. SHERIDAN WAS FURIOUS!

PICKETT HAD REALIZED HOW EXPOSED HIS POSITION WAS AND PULLED BACK IN FRONT OF FIVE FORKS.

LEE WAS JUST AS DISAPPOINTED. HE FELT PICKETT HAD GIVEN UP HIS ADVANTAGE. HE SENT A CURT MESSAGE TO HIM SAYING, "HOLD FIVE FORKS AT ALL HAZARDS."

SHERIDAN NOW INSTRUCTED WARREN TO HIT THE CONFEDERATE LINE ON THEIR LEFT AT A RIGHT ANGLE, WHILE SHERIDAN'S HORSE SOLDIERS WOULD ASSAULT THE FRONT LINE DISMOUNTED.

WARREN'S EXHAUSTED MEN WERE MOVING TOO SLOWLY FOR SHERIDAN, AND IT MADE HIM FURIOUS AS THE DAY WORE ON. HE WAS AFRAID THAT DAYLIGHT WOULD BE GONE BEFORE V CORPS WAS IN POSITION.

THE CONFEDERATE LINE WAS ALSO IN DISARRAY. NO INFANTRY WAS SPOTTED AND PICKETT WAS SURE THEY COULD FIGHT OFF THE CAVALRY.

CONFIDENT OR NONCHALANT, PICKETT, ALONG WITH FITZHUGH LEE AND THOMAS ROSSER, CAUGHT SOME FISH IN A NEARBY STREAM AND HAD A LITTLE FEAST.

AT 4:30 PM, THE FEDERAL INFANTRY HIT THE LEFT FLANK OF THE CONFEDERATE LINE. PICKETT DIDN'T LET ANYONE WHERE HE HAD GONE AND DIDN'T LEAVE ANYONE IN CHARGE. AND HE DIDN'T HEAR THE GUN FIRE EVEN THOUGH HE WAS ONLY A MILE AND A HALF AWAY BECAUSE OF AN ACOUSTIC SHADOW. THE BATTLE BEGAN WITH NO ONE IN CHARGE OF PICKETT'S DIVISION.

THE UNION'S STRATEGY DIDN'T GO AS PLANNED, AND A GAP APPEARED IN THE FEDERAL LINE.

G. K. WARREN SPOTTED THIS MISTAKE AND WHEELED HIS BRIGADE TO THE LEFT TO FILL THE GAP.

THE CONFEDERATES' HEAVY FIRE STRUCK THE FEDERALS, AND THEIR LINE WAVERED.

SUDDENLY, SHERIDAN WAS IN FRONT OF THE RANKS, A SMALL MAN ON A BIG HORSE.

THE CONFEDERATE FIRE WAS DEVASTATING AND MEN WERE BEING CUT DOWN. SHERIDAN WAS RUNNING FROM ONE PART OF THE BATTLE TO ANOTHER, WAVING HIS RED AND WHITE FLAG, "SHAKING HIS FIST, ENCOURAGING, ENTREATING, THREATENING, PRAYING, SWEARING, THE VERY INCARNATION OF BATTLE."

BY THE TIME PICKETT REALIZED WHAT WAS GOING ON, HE FOUND HIMSELF CUT OFF FROM HIS MEN.

BY 6:45 PM, IT WAS ALL OVER. 2,400 CONFEDERATES HAD BEEN CAPTURED, 605 HAD BEEN KILLED AND WOUNDED ALONG WITH 13 FLAGS AND SIX GUNS.

WHEN WORD SPREAD OF THE VICTORY, THE ARMY OF THE POTOMAC SEEMED TO GO WILD WITH CELEBRATION. MEN CHEERED AND SCREAMED UNCONTROLLABLY. THESE SEASONED MEN AND OFFICERS HAD SEEN VICTORY BEFORE, BUT THEY PERHAPS KNEW THAT THIS VICTORY PRESAGED THE END OF THE WAR.

LEE SENT A TELEGRAM TO CONFEDERATE SECRETARY OF WAR JOHN C. BRECKINRIDGE: "I ADVISE THAT ALL PREPARATIONS BE MADE FOR LEAVING RICHMOND TONIGHT."

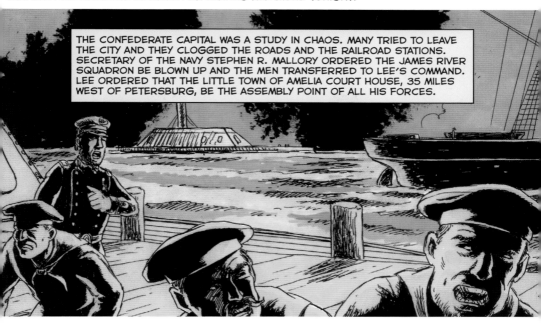

THE CONFEDERATE CAPITAL WAS A STUDY IN CHAOS. MANY TRIED TO LEAVE THE CITY AND THEY CLOGGED THE ROADS AND THE RAILROAD STATIONS. SECRETARY OF THE NAVY STEPHEN R. MALLORY ORDERED THE JAMES RIVER SQUADRON BE BLOWN UP AND THE MEN TRANSFERRED TO LEE'S COMMAND. LEE ORDERED THAT THE LITTLE TOWN OF AMELIA COURT HOUSE, 35 MILES WEST OF PETERSBURG, BE THE ASSEMBLY POINT OF ALL HIS FORCES.

BUT LEE'S FORCES WOULD NEVER REACH AMELIA COURT HOUSE UNLESS PETERSBURG HELD UNTIL NIGHTFALL. SO THE DEFENDERS OF THE INNER LINE OF DEFENSES, FORT GREGG AND BATTERY WHITWORTH, WERE TOLD THEY WOULD HAVE TO HOLD THE DEFENSE AT ALL COST.

NONE OF THE MEMBERS OF THE MISSISSIPPI BRIGADE FLINCHED FROM THIS ALL-IMPORTANT TASK EVEN WHEN THEY WERE OUTNUMBERED 10 TO 1.

TWO OF THE THREE DIVISIONS OF GIBBON'S XXIV CORPS ATTACKED THE DEFENDERS.

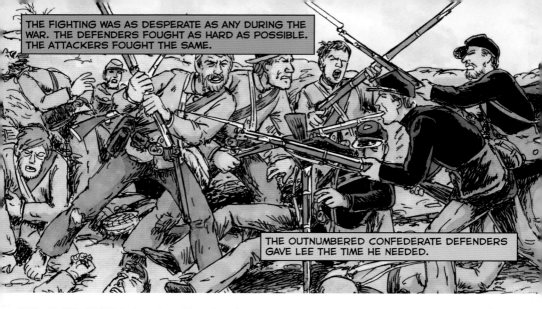

THE FIGHTING WAS AS DESPERATE AS ANY DURING THE WAR. THE DEFENDERS FOUGHT AS HARD AS POSSIBLE. THE ATTACKERS FOUGHT THE SAME.

THE OUTNUMBERED CONFEDERATE DEFENDERS GAVE LEE THE TIME HE NEEDED.

THE CONFEDERATE IRONCLADS AT DREWRY'S BLUFF WERE BLOWN UP. AS A RESULT, REAR ADM. RAPHAEL SEMMES, WHO HAD COMMANDED THE FAMOUS RAIDER *ALABAMA*, NOW BECAME BRIGADIER GENERAL SEMMES AND WOULD LEAD HIS SAILORS AS INFANTRY SOLDIERS., HE WAS ORDERED TO DEFEND DANVILLE.

IN RICHMOND, CONFEDERATE CAVALRY GUARDED THE LAST BRIDGE OVER THE JAMES RIVER. AT DAWN ON APRIL 3, THE LAST CONFEDERATE REAR GUARD CROSSED OVER. BRIGADIER GENERAL MARTIN W. GARY GAVE THE ORDER TO THE COMMANDER OF THE LOCAL MILITIA, CAPTAIN CLEMENT SULIVANE, "ALL OVER, GOOD BYE. BLOW HER TO HELL."

BLACK THURSDAY APRIL 1865

AS UNION FORCES ENTERED RICHMOND, FRAGMENTS OF LEE'S ARMY OF NORTHERN VIRGINIA STRUGGLED TOWARD AMELIA COURT HOUSE. LONGSTREET'S CORPS WAS THE FIRST TO ARRIVE, FOLLOWED BY GORDON, MAHONE, PICKETT, ANDERSON, FITZHUGH LEE AND EWELL'S CAVALRY.

ONE ODD-LOOKING GROUP WAS A BRIGADE OF SAILORS UNDER COMMODORE JOHN R. TUCKER. LEE'S SOLDIERS WERE AMUSED TO HEAR COMMANDS LIKE, "TO THE STARBOARD, MARCH!"

GENERAL LEE HAD ANTICIPATED TO MOVE TO AMELIA COURT HOUSE AND ORDERED THE CONFEDERATE COMMISSARY TO DELIVER 350,000 RATIONS OF BREAD AND MEAT. WHEN SOLDIERS ARRIVED, THEY FOUND NOTHING.

THEY MADE APPEALS TO LOCAL CITIZENS, BUT THEY HAD NOTHING TO GIVE. FORAGE TEAMS WERE SENT OUT TO SCOUT THE LOCAL FARMS AND THEY CAME BACK ALMOST EMPTY-HANDED: THE FARMS HAD ALREADY BEEN STRIPPED THE PREVIOUS WINTER. A FEW MEN WERE ABLE TO FIND A FEW EARS OF CORN INTENDED FOR HORSES. PERCHED OVER AN OPEN FIRE, THE CORN WAS SO HARD IT MADE THEIR JAWS ACHE.

SHERIDAN'S CAVALRY STAYED RIGHT BEHIND THE RETREATING CONFEDERATE ARMY. HUNDREDS OF STRAGGLERS WERE CAPTURED. AND SHERIDAN ORDERED GEORGE CROOK'S DIVISION TO STRIKE SOUTHWEST TO JETERSVILLE. THE IDEA WAS TO GET AHEAD OF LEE'S ARMY.

LEE'S ARMY MARCHED ON, WEAK FROM LACK OF FOOD AND EXHAUSTED FROM HEAVY FIGHTING. LEE TELEGRAPHED AHEAD TO LYNCHBURG, ORDERING FOOD TO BE SENT BY RAIL TO BURKEVILLE. MEN DREAMED OF THE FOOD THAT THEY PRAYED WOULD BE WAITING FOR THEM. THEY MARCHED ON THROUGH A HEAVY RAIN ON APRIL 5, STARVED AND UTTERLY EXHAUSTED.

"WE STOPPED FOR WHAT WAS TO BE THE MIDDAY MEAL," A CONFEDERATE OFFICER RECALLED. "THE MIDDAY WAS THERE, BUT THE MEAL WAS NOT." WAGONS CARRYING ITEMS LIKE COOKING UTENSILS, FRYING PANS, AND KETTLES WERE LEFT BEHIND. WRITTEN ON THE SIDE OF ONE ABANDONED WAGON WAS A SARCASTIC MESSAGE:

THE BLUE CAVALRY WOULD OCCASIONALLY SKIRMISH WITH THE RETREATING REBELS. DESPITE THEIR WEAKENED CONDITION, THE SOUTHERN SOLDIERS FOUGHT FIERCELY.

WHEN LONGSTREET REACHED RICE'S STATION MIDMORNING ON THURSDAY, APRIL 6, HE FOUND THAT SEVERAL HUNDRED FEDERAL CAVALRYMEN AND SEVERAL YANKEE INFANTRY REGIMENTS HAD PASSED THROUGH AHEAD OF THEM.

LONGSTREET WAS EXTREMELY ALARMED. HE DIRECTED 1,200 CONFEDERATE CAVALRYMEN UNDER GEN. THOMAS ROSSER TO PURSUE AND DESTROY THE FEDERAL FORCE IF IT TOOK THE LAST MAN OF HIS COMMAND TO DO IT.

LONGSTREET KNEW WHAT THE YANKEE CAVALRYMEN WERE AFTER: THE SO-CALLED HIGH BRIDGE, WHICH SPANNED A FLOOD PLAIN OF THE APPOMATTOX RIVER. THE BRIDGE WAS A HALF-MILE LONG AND 126 FEET HIGH. IF IT WAS DESTROYED, LEE'S ARMY WOULD BE TRAPPED.

THE CONFEDERATES CAUGHT UP WITH THE FEDERALS AROUND NOON, BEFORE THEY HAD A CHANCE TO DESTROY THE BRIDGE. A DESPERATE HAND-TO-HAND FIGHT ENSUED.

THE CONFEDERATES OVERWHELMED THE UNION CAVALRYMEN, INFLICTING MANY CASUALTIES AND TAKING MORE THAN 60 PRISONERS. WITH THE UNION CAVALRY OUT OF THE WAY, THEY THEN DEALT WITH THE INFANTRY, WHICH HAD TAKEN A POSITION ON A NEARBY HILL.

ROSSER'S CAVALRYMEN DROVE THE YANKEE INFANTRY FROM THE HILL. CONFUSED AND IN THE OPEN, THEY SURRENDERED IN MASS. 800 PRISONERS WERE CAPTURED, ALONG WITH SIX COLORS AND GUIDONS AND A COMPLETE BRASS BAND.

LEE KEPT THE HEAD OF THE COLUMN MOVING, WHICH CAUSED THE ARMY TO BE OVERSTRECHED.

SHERIDAN'S CAVALRY CONSTANTLY ATTACKED THE REAR AND FLANKS.

AROUND NOON ON APRIL 6, RICHARD ANDERSON SENT A COLUMN OF WAGONS DOWN A ROAD THAT FORKED TO THE NORTH TO PROTECT THEM FROM FEDERAL CAVALRY LED BY GEORGE ARMSTRONG CUSTER. GORDON'S FORCES, WHO WERE TAKING UP THE REAR, FOLLOWED THE WAGONS, THINKING THIS WAS THE MAIN ROUTE OF THE ARMY.

THE REMAINDER OF THE CORPS OF ANDERSON AND EWELL CONTINUED ON THE MAIN ROAD. AFTER ANDERSON'S MEN CROSSED SAILOR'S CREEK, THEY FOUND ALL THREE OF SHERIDAN'S CAVALRY DIVISIONS BLOCKING THE ROAD AHEAD OF THEM AND ON THE HIGH GROUND TO THEIR LEFT.

WORSE STILL, ELEMENTS OF WRIGHT'S SIXTH CORPS WERE COMING IN FROM THE NORTH AGAINST EWELL'S REAR.

FROM THE VALLEY OF LITTLE CREEK, EWELL'S MEN WATCHED AS THE SIXTH CORPS DEPLOYED THEIR INFANTRY AND CANNON AROUND THE HILLSMAN HOUSE BEHIND THEM. THE CONFEDERATES BEGAN TO BUILD WHAT FIELD WORKS THEY COULD ON THE SOUTHWESTERN SIDE OF THE CREEK. THEY WERE OUTNUMBERED MORE THAN TWO TO ONE.

A LITTLE AFTER 5 PM, THE FEDERAL ARTILLERY OPENED UP AND THEIR INFANTRY BEGAN TO ADVANCE ACROSS THE SOGGY CREEK BED.

THE FIGHTING WAS FIERCE. THE REBELS MOUNTED A SMALL COUNTERATTACK LED BY THE 18TH GEORGIA BATTALION AND SOME ARTILLERYMAN WITHOUT THEIR CANNON, WHICH DROVE THE FEDERAL CENTER BACK ACROSS THE CREEK.

BUT THERE WERE JUST TOO MANY OF THEM.

THE UNION'S NUMBERS DISSECTED THE CONFEDERATE LINE, AND THE BATTLE DEGENERATED INTO A CONFUSED MELEE OF SMALL, BLOODY FIGHTS. MANY REBELS BROKE AND RAN. YET SOME SMALL GROUPS SURROUNDED THEIR COLORS AND FOUGHT UNTIL ANNIHILATED.

THE REMAINING MEN OF THE 18TH GEORGIA BATTALION, THE SAVANNAH VOLUNTEER GUARD, FOUGHT UNTIL ITS COMPLETE DESTRUCTION. THEY WERE NOT THE LAST.

SOME OF THE LAST TO GIVE UP WERE WHAT WAS LEFT OF COMMODORE TUCKER'S SAILORS.

THE UNION VICTORY WAS COMPLETE. EWELL'S CORPS WAS DESTROYED AND ANDERSON'S WAS AT LEAST HALVED. 2,000 MEN WERE KILLED, WOUNDED, OR SCATTERED, AND 6,000 WERE CAPTURED. EIGHT GENERALS, INCLUDING EWELL AND LEE'S SON CUSTIS, WERE ALSO CAPTURED. WHEN LEE SAW THE SURVIVORS STREAMING DOWN THE ROAD, HE COMMENTED, "MY GOD! HAS THE ARMY BEEN DISSOLVED?"

VALOR & DEVOTION

IN THE EARLY MORNING HOURS OF APRIL 7, 1865, UNION TROOPS ARRIVED AT THE HIGH BRIDGE OVER THE APPOMATTOX RIVER JUST AS CONFEDERATE FORCES WERE ATTEMPTING TO BURN IT. REBEL SHARPSHOOTERS TRIED TO HOLD THE ENEMY BACK, BUT THE FEDERALS WERE ABLE TO CAPTURE IT, SAVING ALL BUT FOUR SPANS OF THE HIGH BRIDGE AND THE ENTIRE WAGON BRIDGE THAT RAN BELOW IT.

ALL THAT DAY, UNION FORCES MARCHED FORWARD, TIRED BUT IN HIGH SPIRITS. IN THE EVENING THEY PASSED GRANT SITTING ON THE PORCH OF THE PRINCE EDWARD HOTEL IN FARMVILLE.

THAT EVENING AT 5PM GRANT WROTE A SHORT NOTE TO BE SENT TO LEE: "THE RESULTS OF THE LAST WEEK MUST CONVINCE YOU OF THE HOPELESSNESS OF FURTHER RESISTANCE ON THE PART OF THE ARMY OF NORTHERN VIRGINIA. I FEEL THAT IT IS SO, AND REGARD IT AS MY DUTY TO SHIFT FROM MYSELF THE RESPONSIBILITY OF ANY FURTHER EFFUSION OF BLOOD, BY ASKING OF YOU THE SURRENDER OF THAT PORTION OF THE CONFEDERATE STATES ARMY KNOWN AS THE ARMY OF NORTHERN VIRGINIA."

BEFORE THEM WAS A SEA OF BLUE: THE ENTIRE ARMY OF THE JAMES, GIBBON'S XXIV CORPS, AND A DIVISION OF UNITED STATES COLORED TROOPS FROM XXV CORPS.

THE ARMIES CONTINUED TO SKIRMISH UNTIL GORDON SENT A MESSAGE TO LEE: "I HAVE FOUGHT MY CORPS TO A FRAZZLE, AND I FEAR I CAN DO NOTHING UNLESS I AM HEAVILY SUPPORTED BY LONGSTREET'S CORPS." AT THIS, LEE KNEW WHAT HE HAD TO DO. "THERE IS NOTHING LEFT FOR ME BUT TO GO AND SEE GENERAL GRANT, AND I'D RATHER DIE A THOUSAND DEATHS."

AT 8:30 AM, LEE MOUNTED TRAVELLER AND RODE EAST TO MEET GRANT. WITH HIM WERE COL. W. H. TAYLOR AND COL. CHARLES MARSHALL AND SGT. G. W. TUCKER.

THERE WAS STILL FIGHTING GOING ON. ONE OF THE CASUALTIES OF CONFEDERATE ARTILLERY FIRE WAS PVT. WILLIAM MONTGOMERY OF THE 155TH PENNSYLVANIA ZOAVES. FOR MANY YEARS IT WAS THOUGHT THAT HE WAS ONLY 15 YEARS OLD, BUT FAMILY RECORDS NOW PROVE HE WAS 19. HE WAS MORTALLY WOUNDED AND DIED TWO WEEKS LATER IN A FARMVILLE HOSPITAL.

IT WASN'T AN EASY TASK FOR THE GENERALS TO MAKE CONTACT WITH ONE ANOTHER. GENERAL MEADE AGREED TO A ONE-HOUR TRUCE WHILE COURIERS RACED AFTER GRANT.

THE FRAGILE TRUCE NEARLY FELL APART WHEN CUSTER APPROACHED LONGSTREET AND SAID, "IN THE NAME OF GENERAL SHERIDAN, I DEMAND THE UNCONDITIONAL SURRENDER OF THIS ARMY."

LONGSTREET EXPLODED, INFORMING CUSTER, "THAT I WAS NOT THE COMMANDER OF THE ARMY, THAT HE WAS WITHIN THE LINES OF THE ENEMY WITHOUT AUTHORITY, ADDRESSING A SUPERIOR OFFICER, AND IN DISRESPECT TO GENERAL GRANT AS WELL AS MYSELF."

WHEN CUSTER LEFT HE TOLD LONGSTREET THAT HE WOULD "BE RESPONSIBLE FOR THE BLOODSHED TO FOLLOW." LONGSTREET SNAPPED, "GO AHEAD AND HAVE ALL THE BLOODSHED YOU WANT."

A LITTLE AFTER 11 AM, A UNION COURIER FOUND GRANT AND HIS STAFF RESTING IN A CLEARING. GRANT WAS SUFFERING FROM A HEADACHE THAT HAD PLAGUED HIM FOR NEARLY A DAY. THE COURIER HAD A LETTER FROM LEE, REQUESTING "A SUSPENSION OF HOSTILITIES PENDING THE ADJUSTMENT OF THE TERMS OF THE SURRENDER OF THIS ARMY."

GRANT READ THE LETTER SILENTLY. HE THEN HANDED IT OVER TO JOHN RAWLINS, HIS CHIEF OF STAFF, TO READ ALOUD.

RAWLINS READ THE NOTE FOR EVERYONE. THERE WAS SILENCE. SOMEONE STARTED TO CHEER, BUT IT ENDED FEEBLY. A FEW EMBRACED EACH OTHER. GRANT FELT WONDERFUL. THE HEADACHE WAS GONE.

LEE SENT CHARLES MARSHALL INTO APPOMATTOX COURTHOUSE TO FIND A SUITABLE PLACE TO MEET GRANT.

MARSHALL APPROACHED WILMER MCLEAN, WHO OWNED THE MOST PROSPEROUS-LOOKING HOME IN TOWN. MCLEAN HAD ONCE LIVED WITH HIS FAMILY AT MANASSAS JUNCTION, AND HIS HOUSE THERE HAD SUFFERED DAMAGE DURING FIRST BULL RUN. HE HAD MOVED TO APPOMATTOX DURING THE WAR. NOW IT HAD CAUGHT UP WITH HIM AGAIN.

LEE ARRIVED AT THE MCLEAN RESIDENCE AT 1 PM WEARING HIS BEST UNIFORM AND HIS FINEST SWORD. GRANT ARRIVED ABOUT A HALF HOUR LATER. GRANT AND HIS STAFF WERE MUD SPLATTERED AFTER RIDING TWENTY TWO MILES THAT DAY. HE HAD HIS FIELD GLASSES SLUNG ACROSS HIS SHOULDERS BUT HAD NO SWORD.

IN THE MCLEAN PARLOR WERE ROBERT E. LEE, CHARLES MARSHALL, ULYSSES S. GRANT, PHILIP SHERIDAN, ORVILLE BABCOCK, HORACE PORTER, EDWARD O. C. ORD, SETH WILLIAMS, THEODORE BOWERS, ELY PARKER, RUFUS INGALLS, AND CAPT. ROBERT TODD LINCOLN, THE PRESIDENT'S SON. AS GRANT ENTERED THE ROOM, LEE ROSE TO HIS FEET AND THEY SHOOK HANDS.

GRANT FOUND HIMSELF SAD AND DEPRESSED, RATHER THAN JOYFUL OVER THIS VICTORY. CONSEQUENTLY, HE BEGAN CHATTING WITH LEE, TALKING ABOUT THEIR EXPERIENCES IN THE MEXICAN WAR IN THE OLD ARMY.

LEE QUIETLY BROUGHT GRANT BACK TO THE POINT OF THEIR MEETING: "I SUPPOSE, GENERAL GRANT, THAT THE OBJECT OF OUR PRESENT MEETING IS FULLY UNDERSTOOD. I ASKED TO SEE YOU TO ASCERTAIN UPON WHAT TERMS YOU WOULD RECEIVE THE SURRENDER OF MY ARMY."

GRANT EXPLAINED THE TERMS: "THE OFFICERS AND MEN SURRENDERING TO BE PAROLED AND DISQUALIFIED FROM TAKING UP ARMS UNTIL PROPERLY EXCHANGED, AND ALL ARMS, AMMUNITION AND SUPPLIES TO BE DELIVERED UP AS CAPTURED PROPERLY."

THESE TERMS WERE WRITTEN OUT AND EXPANDED UPON: "THE OFFICERS AND MEN WILL BE ALLOWED TO RETURN TO THEIR HOMES, NOT TO BE DISTURBED BY THE UNITED STATES AUTHORITY SO LONG AS THEY OBSERVE THEIR PAROLES AND THE LAWS IN FORCE WHERE THEY MAY RESIDE."

THE TERMS WERE VERY GENEROUS, AND LEE WAS QUITE PLEASED.

BUT THERE WAS SOMETHING ELSE ON LEE'S MIND. "THE CAVALRYMEN AND ARTILLERIST OWN THEIR OWN HORSES IN OUR ARMY. I WOULD LIKE TO UNDERSTAND WHETHER THESE MEN WILL BE PERMITTED TO RETAIN THEIR HORSES."

"THIS WILL HAVE THE BEST POSSIBLE EFFECT ON THE MEN," LEE RESPONDED. "IT WILL BE VERY GRATIFYING AND WILL DO MUCH TOWARD CONCILIATING OUR PEOPLE."

LEE INDICATED THAT THEY HAD ABOUT A THOUSAND FEDERAL PRISONERS WHO HE WANTED TO RETURN AS SOON AS POSSIBLE, AS THEY COULD NOT FEED THEM. "I HAVE, INDEED, NOTHING FOR MY OWN MEN."

GRANT THOUGHT OF THE MATTER AND AFTER A LITTLE CONSIDERATION HE AMENDED HIS TERMS: "I WILL INSTRUCT THE OFFICERS AND I SHALL APPOINT TO RECEIVE THE PAROLES TO LET ALL THE MEN WHO CLAIM TO OWN A HORSE OR A MULE TO TAKE THEIR ANIMALS HOME WITH THEM TO WORK THEIR LITTLE FARMS."

NOW THAT THE TERMS WERE AGREED UPON, GRANT ASKED THEODORE BOWERS TO COPY THE ORDER IN INK. BOWERS WAS SO NERVOUS OVER THE GRAVITY OF THE SITUATION, HE COULD NOT WRITE STEADILY. ELY PARKER, A SENECA INDIAN CHIEF, TOOK OVER.

GRANT ACCEPTED THE RETURN OF THE PRISONERS AND ISSUED ORDERS FOR RATIONS TO BE SHARED WITH THE DEFEATED CONFEDERATES.

WHEN LEE CAME BACK OUT ON THE MCLEAN PORCH, THE FEDERAL OFFICERS IN THE YARD CAME TO ATTENTION AND SALUTED, WHICH LEE RETURNED.

THE LETTERS WERE EXCHANGED AT 3 PM.

AS LEE CLIMBED ONTO TRAVELLER'S SADDLE, GRANT REMOVED HIS HAT. THE OTHER FEDERAL OFFICERS DID THE SAME. LEE RAISED HIS HAT IN RETURN AND THEN SLOWLY RODE BACK TO HIS ARMY.

AS SOON AS THE WORD OF THE SURRENDER REACHED HIM, GEORGE MEADE JUMPED ON HIS HORSE. HE HAD BEEN SICK WITH STOMACH TROUBLES FOR THE PAST SEVERAL DAYS AND HAD HARDLY LEFT HIS AMBULANCE. BUT NOW THAT SEEMED UNIMPORTANT. HE RODE THROUGH THE UNION CAMP SHOUTING, "IT'S ALL OVER, BOYS! LEE SURRENDERED! IT'S ALL OVER!"

THE UNION CAMP ERUPTED WITH JOY. IT WAS ONE MASS CELEBRATION WITH LOTS OF REJOICING.

AS LEE RODE BACK TO HIS CAMP, HIS MEN GATHERED AROUND HIM. "ARE WE SURRENDERED?" SOMEONE ASKED. LEE'S VOICE TREMBLED, AND HIS CHEEKS WERE WET WITH TEARS. "MEN, WE HAVE FOUGHT THE WAR TOGETHER, AND I HAVE DONE THE BEST I COULD FOR YOU. YOU WILL BE PAROLED AND GO TO YOUR HOMES UNTIL EXCHANGED." TEARS FILLED HIS EYES, AND HE FINALLY SAID, "GOODBYE."

"GENERAL, WE'LL FIGHT 'EM YET," ONE SOLDIER SAID. "SAY THE WORD AND WE'LL GO IN AND FIGHT 'EM YET."

BUT THE REALITY SUNK IN. MOST RESPONDED IN SILENCE.

EXCEPT ONE MAN. HE THREW HIS RIFLE DOWN AND CRIED OUT IN A LOUD VOICE, "BLOW, GABRIEL, BLOW! MY GOD, LET HIM BLOW, I AM READY TO DIE!" A RAGGED SOLDIER STOOD BESIDE HIS COMMANDER. "I LOVE YOU JUST AS WELL AS EVER, GENERAL LEE."

ON THE MORNING OF WEDNESDAY, APRIL 12, THE 28,231 REMAINING SOLDIERS OF THE ARMY OF NORTHERN VIRGINIA MARCHED TOWARD THE UNION CAMP. THROUGH BATTLE, THE REBEL UNITS HAD SO SHRUNK IN SIZE THAT THE NUMBER OF THEIR BATTLE FLAGS SEEMED ODD. THE CRIMSON FLAGS WERE, AS JOSHUA LAWRENCE CHAMBERLAIN SAID, "CROWDED SO THICK, BY THINNING OUT OF MEN, THAT THE WHOLE COLUMN SEEMED CROWNED WITH RED."

BETWEEN TWO LINES OF FEDERAL TROOPS, THEY STACKED THEIR ARMS AND "LASTLY—AND RELUCTANTLY, WITH AGONY OF EXPRESSION—THEY FOLD THEIR FLAGS, BATTLE-WORN AND TORN, BLOOD-STAINED, HEART-HOLDING COLORS, AND LAY THEM DOWN."

THEN THEY WENT HOME. THE FORTUNATE ONES WERE ABLE TO TRAVEL BY RAIL OR STEAMSHIP FOR AT LEAST PART OF THEIR JOURNEY. A FEW, MOSTLY FORMER CAVALRYMEN, HAD THE BENEFIT OF A HORSE OR MULE. BUT MOST WENT HOME AS THEY HAD FOUGHT, ON FOOT. MANY OF THEM HAD JOURNEYS OF MANY HUNDREDS OF MILES AND IT WAS MANY MONTHS BEFORE THEY SAW THEIR HOMES AND LOVED ONES.

THE GREAT MEN WENT HOME TOO.

Fort Sumter National Monument
1214 Middle Street • Sullivan's Island, SC 29482
www.nps.gov/fosu

Gettysburg National Military Park
1195 Baltimore Pike, Suite 1000 • Gettysburg, PA 17325
www.nps.gov/gett

Kennesaw Mountain National Battlefield Park
900 Kennesaw Mountain Drive [a] Kennesaw, GA 30152
www.nps.gov/kemo

Manassas National Battlefield Park
12521 Lee Highway • Manassas, VA 20109
www.nps.gov.mana

Monocacy National Battlefield
5201 Urbana Pike • Frederick, MD 21704
www.nps.gov/mono

Pea Ridge National Military Park
15930 East Highway 62 • Garfield, AR 72732
www.nps.gov/peri

Shiloh National Military Park
1055 Pittsburg Landing Road • Shiloh, TN 38376
www.nps.gov/shil

Stones Rivers National Battlefield
3501 Old Nashville Highway • Murfreesboro, TN 37129
www.nps.gov/stri

Vicksburg National Military Park
3201 Clay Street • Vicksburg, MS 39183
www.nps.gov/vick

Wilson's Creek National Battlefield
6424 West Farm Road 182 • Republic, MO 65738
ww.nps.gov/wicr

About the Author

WRITER AND ARTIST WAYNE VANSANT WAS THE PRIMARY ARTIST FOR MARVEL'S *THE 'NAM* FOR MORE THAN FIVE YEARS. SINCE THEN, HE HAS WRITTEN AND ILLUSTRATED MANY HISTORICALLY ACCURATE BOOKS SUCH AS *ANTIETAM: THE FIERY TRIAL* (WITH THE NATIONAL PARK SERVICE); *THE VIETNAM WAR: A GRAPHIC HISTORY*; *NORMANDY: A GRAPHIC HISTORY OF D-DAY, THE ALLIED INVASION OF HITLER'S FORTRESS EUROPE*; AND *GETTYSBURG: THE GRAPHIC HISTORY OF AMERICA'S MOST FAMOUS BATTLE AND THE TURNING POINT OF THE CIVIL WAR*. HE IS CURRENTLY WORKING ON A GRAPHIC HISTORY OF MANFRED VON RICHTHOFEN, AKA THE RED BARON, FOR ZENITH PRESS (2014).